Copyright © 2014 by Rev. Henry Aikondion Idonije

All rights reserved. No part of this publication may be reproduced, distributed, or transmitted in any form or by any means, including photocopying, recording, or other electronic or mechanical methods, without the prior written permission of the author, except in the case of brief quotations embodied in critical reviews and certain other noncommercial uses permitted by copyright law.

Printed and bound in Canada at McNally Robinson Booksellers
1120 Grant Avenue, Winnipeg, Manitoba R3M 2A6.

Cover and Book design by McNally Robinson Booksellers.

www.mcnallyrobinson.com/selfpublishing

ISBN 978-1-928169-40-6

First Edition October 2014

THE CHURCH

MATT.16:18

AN ORGANISM BUILT BY
CHRIST AND NOT MAN

Rev. Henry A. Idonije

CONTENTS

	Dedication	7
	Endorsement	9
	Introduction	11
Chapter 1	Christ & His Church	15
Chapter 2	Thirteen Apostles & What Became of Them	23
Chapter 3	I Am of The Church	46
Chapter 4	With You, It Shall Not be So	50
Chapter 5	Biblical Definition & The Purpose of the Church..	62
Chapter 6	God's Tabernacle	76
Chapter 7	You Are Invincible	80
Chapter 8	The Church: An Overcomer	85
Chapter 9	Christ Talks to His Church	89
Chapter 10	The First Hundred Years of His Church	94
Chapter 11	Bad Eggs in His Church	101
Chapter 12	The Church As She Was & How She Lived	108
Chapter 13	The Scriptures & the Church	113
Chapter 14	Elders & Bishops Are the Same	119
Chapter 15	Five Fold Ministries Given to His Church	123
Chapter 16	God's Spirit Working with His Church	141
Chapter 17	Alternative Ways of Having Church	145
Chapter 18	Basic Principle of the New Testament Church	148
Chapter 19	God & Building	152
Chapter 20	House Church Fellowships	156
Chapter 21	Organism & Organizations (Parts: 1-3)	168
Chapter 22	The Progression of the Church	202
Chapter 23	The Church: An Organism	229
	Conclusion	237
	Autobiography	243

DEDICATION

I dedicate this book to the billions of the saints of God who are working under God unnoticed, unseen, and unappreciated all over the world. I say well done, and thank you for your commitment and tenacity in holding on to the Lord.

I dedicate it to the ministers and saints who know the One that is building the Church, and have submitted to Christ's leadership, ownership, and have received of His humility, having learned of Him, and heeded His call in Matt.11:30.

I dedicate it to my family and dear friends from whom I have come to understand that the Church is made up of individual families in God, as we share our lives together in relationship, in the midst of conflicts, triumphs and trials.

And finally, I dedicate it to the Father, who gave of Himself through His Son, Jesus Christ to redeem us from the wrath to come, and from the power of darkness. To His Son, Jesus Christ, who is our Triumph and Champion, the Conqueror of hell, our Magnificent Obsession, and the One who had the power over Satan and demons. He is the Way, the Truth and the Life, paving the way for the saints to the Celestial City, leading us to His Father.

ENDORSEMENT

DR. ISRAEL IDONIJE

The issues raised in this book concern the word CHURCH as to whether she is an organism or organization. Is she a product of God or man? Is she made out of bricks, cement, nails, water, glass and material things? Men are building Churches, but are they instructed of the Lord? Are cathedrals, mega churches, huge buildings, and great mansions qualify as the Church? Henry Idonije gave us a perspective from the divine angle of what the Church is by His definition.

I have known my father, Henry A Idonije, as a man, philanthropist, writer, and minister of the Word of God for over thirty years. I am proud to have seen him in close quarters in all of the years that he served the people of Brandon, Winnipeg, and the surrounding communities.

He has an understanding from the Lord as to who the Church is, and thus he is able to give credit to God, through His Son, Jesus Christ, the Owner and Builder of His Church. The Church is the gathering of God's people, and He tabernacles among them. The Scriptures say, "Behold the Tabernacle of God is with men…" (Rev.21:3ff)

One thing I noticed about him is his resiliency, commitment, dedication and tenacity to whatever he believed God has committed into his care. He has excelled in all the areas of his life as they relate to people, ministry, family and the call of God. He wants the world to know that the Church is not a physical structure, but an organism, being built by the Lord Himself.

I am an ardent supporter, and a fan of his works and ministry. He carries this dependability, consistency, and tenacity into all the areas and walks of life. God has shown and done many amazing things in his life. This fuels his commitment and the determination to see God's work passed on to others. He is very determined to see God's glory fulfilled in his life, and in the lives of those around him.

He is a loving father and dedicated servant of the Lord. He is always for the truth, regardless of his opinions. He served in the ministry for over thirty years, and as a retired elder-man, he is opening his heart to share all that the Lord has done in and through him for the younger generations still to come.

He has written five books, and this is his sixth one. This book will give believers insight as to who "THE CHURCH" is, and who is building her? I recommend "THE CHURCH" to all those who are seeking the truth as to who is responsible for the birth of the Church? Jesus Christ said, "I Will Build My Church, And The Gates Of Hell Will Not Prevail Against Her."

My father has served as a Chaplain to the Brandon Police Service, was a Treasurer to the Brandon Ministerial Association, Chaplain to the Brotherhood of Railway Association in Brandon, he served for twenty-two years in feeding the hungry and homeless of Brandon, pastored Tabernacle of the Lord's Fellowship for twenty years, received the Canadian Caring Award, the Order of Manitoba, and other citations.

Dr. Israel I Idonije: LL. D, O.M.
NFL: Defensive Lineman
(Chicago Bears 2012)

INTRODUCTION

God is one hundred percent Spirit, and not flesh and blood, but man is both spirit and body. Anything therefore that He makes, in terms of reproducing Himself, must be spiritual as well, with blood in man for his redemption. He made the outer, physical man out of the dust of the ground, and sculptured him into a shape like Himself, but it was lifeless. He breathed a part of Himself into the nostril of the formless structure of the ground, and man became a living being, just like His Maker and Creator. In order for God's Spirit to live on earth, He must put His Spirit inside a body, hence the dust of the earth, containing His Spirit. This was the Spirit's first advent into our world.

The dust of the earth contained God's Spirit, but man did not pass the probationary period of his existence on earth. His clay body could not be amalgamated with the Spirit within. He fell, and His Spirit was housed in a corrupt body, but the plans for His Spirit in man remained. This plan pointed to the redemption of man by His Son, Jesus Christ.

The reason why Christ came was to retrieve that eternal Spirit of God in man to be part of His Being forever as it was in the beginning. Death must occur if Christ was to be man's propitiation for sin. Hence, the cross of Calvary that Christ died on to secure eternity for those who will come to God through Him.

At the climax of His Life on earth, He spilled all of His blood, and became eternally, the Way, Life and Truth in God, and to God. Hence Christ said, "I will build My Church, and the gates of hell shall not prevail against her." (Matt.16:18) Therefore, if Christ is the One building His Church, He too must build something that is not of this world, but of heaven and spiritual. This brings us to conclude that the Church cannot be made of sand, mortal, nails, glass, woods, cement, iron and all the decorations of our 21st century.

Christ came: 1) To retrieve the deposit of God in man. 2) To destroy the works of Satan, the ruler of darkness. 3) To set mankind free from the grip of Satan. (Lk.4:18-19) 4) To bring mankind to God through Himself, having abolished the enmity between God and man.

In Christendom, the ministers of God knew that the Church is organic, and the builder is Christ, the Lord. But their reality denies this, because of power and money. It began in the 2nd century, and the stage was set for the organization of the body of Christ. Ministers ordained others and themselves as apostles, bishops, archbishops, archdeacons, doctors and pope by those who had become mega ministers, and the race for the organization began.

The Bishops ignore the first century set up, and they formed their own hierarchy, thus began the organization of Churches, and the denominations took on the name of the Church. When humans prefixed their declaration by, "God Told Me" who is man to go against Him. The proliferation of Churches started, and the world today has over three billion inorganic churches known as denominations. The quest for money, popularity, power and recognition drove ministers to unparalleled heights in their services as they came up with many strange things removed from the 1st century, when Christ walked the earth with His disciples and saints.

The writer of this book believes that denominations are abomination to God, and through it, the word of God is negated for the denominational traditions. Hierarchies were set up, and the race for all kinds of titles, honors, names, designations and offices began. Even though they said in their hearts that the Church is organic, they denied it in the functioning and practices of their actions, and they promoted their denominations as organizations above the word of God.

Chapter One

CHRIST AND HIS CHURCH

JOHNNY ELMORE
By Permission

The apostle Paul wrote in Eph.5:23-32, "For the husband is the head of the wife, even as Christ is the head of the Church: and he is the Savior of the body. Therefore, as the Church is subject unto Christ, so let the wives be to their own husbands in every thing. Husbands, love your wives, even as Christ also loved the Church, and gave himself for her; that he might sanctify and cleanse her with the washing of water by the word, that he might present her to himself a glorious Church, not having spot, or wrinkle, or any such thing; but that she should be holy and without blemish. So ought men to love their wives as their own bodies. He that loves his wife loves himself. For no man ever yet hated his own flesh; but nourishes and cherishes it, even as the Lord the Church: For we are members of his body, of his flesh, and of his bones. For this cause shall a man leave his father and mother, and shall be joined unto his wife, and they two shall be one flesh. This is a great mystery: but I speak concerning Christ and the Church."

In this passage, we ought to be able to see and appreciate the close relationship that exists between Christ and the Church. The close affinity between Christ and the Church is suggested by the figure of the relationship between husband and wife.

It was predicted by Isaiah that God would give in his house "a place and a name" better than that of "sons and of daughters". (Isa.56:5) We are told in ITim.3:15 that God's House is the "Church of the living God." The term "wife" is suggestive of a closer tie and a more divine union than "sons and daughters." As the husband is the head of the wife, Paul said that even so is Christ the head of the Church.

Therefore, the apostle Paul suggests in Eph.5:23 that the husband is Christ, and the wife is the Church. Just as a husband and a wife become one, and forsake all and any others, and blend their lives into a oneness and unity, in the same way, a Christian is to forsake everything else, divorce himself from everything that would hinder, and blend his life into the life of the Lord Jesus Christ. The husband is Christ, and we, as members of the Church, make up the wife, or the bride of Christ. The marriage relationship that results is the Church of Christ is under the headship of Jesus Christ, our Lord.

I also believe there is an analogy between the first woman who ever lived on the earth, mother Eve, and her husband, Adam, and the Church of Christ in its relationship to Jesus Christ, our Lord.

The Bible declares in the second chapter of Genesis, that after all the things of the earth had been created, the beasts of the field, the fish of the sea, and the fowls of the air, all these various things were brought to Adam to see by what name he would call them. When Adam had named all the beasts of the field, and all the fowls of the air, the Creator was conscious of the fact that every animal and every fowl had its respective mate, and then God looked at man, and said, "It is not good." Up until that moment, God's pronouncement had been not only that things were good, but that they were very good. But now God came to a point in the development of creation in which he said, "It is not good." What was it that was "not good"? He said: "It is not good that the man should be alone". (Gen.2:18) Probably there are a number of women, young and old, who would agree with that statement, and they are right.

God said that it was not good for man to be alone, and he said: "I will make an help meet for him." I might point out that the term "help meet" means "suitable companion." In accord with God's determination to make a help meet for Adam, the last, greatest and highest of all creation was brought into existence when God created mother Eve.

I want to show that the means God used in bringing about the creation of Adam's wife, formed a fitting analogy to the establishment, creation, and formation of the Church of Christ, which was to be the bride of the second Adam, Jesus Christ. What did God do? The Bible says: "And the Lord God caused a deep sleep to fall upon Adam, and he slept". (Gen.2:21)

After God had caused Adam to sleep, he opened his side, and what a wonderful thing that suggests. The woman was not taken from Adam's head, that she might rule over him, nor from his feet, that he might trample upon her, but from out of his side, that she might be a partner and companion along the pathway of life. Then what happened?

The Bible says, "And he took one of his ribs, and closed up the flesh instead thereof." (Gen.2:21) That which was to form the woman was taken from Adam's side – a rib. Therefore, Adam paid the price, the price of his flesh and bone for the one who was to be his companion and helpmeet.

The woman was then created out of the material taken from his side. The Bible states: "And the rib, which the Lord God had taken from man, made he a woman". (Gen.2:22)

The woman was then given to Adam to be his wife, to take upon herself his name, to be married to him. The Bible says that God "brought her unto the man. And Adam said, "This is now bone of my bones, and flesh of my flesh: she shall be called woman, because she was taken out of man". (Gen.2:22, 23)

As a natural result of that union, children began to be born of that first pair, and the earth was to be replenished as a result. Rehearsing that account just briefly, we can say that Adam was at first alone, but God said that was not good. God determined to make a help meet, a suitable companion, for him. Therefore, Adam was put to sleep, his side was opened and the rib was taken from his side, the woman was created, and became Adam's wife, and as a result, children would be born and replenish the earth.

I believe that from that very simple story concerning the creation of woman, the first woman, we can draw a very beautiful analogy to the creation of the Church of the Lord Jesus Christ. God planned in his great wisdom that at the proper time, when man was ready to receive the truth, the Church was to be formed. And just as Adam was the head of the woman, or the wife, so Christ was to be the head of the Church. Therefore, we may expect to find a fitting parallel in the establishment of the Church.

Do you remember what God did first in creating the woman? He caused a deep sleep to come upon Adam. Now look at the first thing he did in forming the spiritual wife, the Lamb's bride.

After Jesus had lived for thirty-three years upon the earth, and had fulfilled the prophecies concerning him, he was taken at last and nailed to the cross. While suspended upon the cross from the third hour of the day until the ninth hour, during the last three hours, a great darkness fell upon the face of the earth. It seems to me that God himself veiled his face and refused to look upon the greatest tragedy of all ages, which was being carried out.

The record says that finally, the sinless Son of God bowed his head upon his guileless bosom, and yielded up the ghost, declaring: "It is finished." While Jesus slept the deep sleep of death, a Roman soldier pierced his side with a spear, opening up the literal flesh of the body of Jesus, and in harmony with the creation of woman, there came forth from the side of Jesus that which was to purchase the Church of Christ. The Bible says: "And forthwith came there out blood and water". (Jn.19:34) Therefore, Christ shed his blood, and with that made the sacrifice, and gave his blood that he might purchase and buy the institution that was to be his spiritual bride, or the wife of the Son of God.

The apostle Paul said: "Take heed therefore unto yourselves, and to all the flock, over the which the Holy Ghost has made you overseers, to feed the Church of God, which he hath purchased with his own blood". (Acts.20:28)

Look at what happened in the formation of the Church. God caused the sleep of death to fall upon Jesus. The material to build the Church was taken from his side. Jesus paid with his blood. The Church, the Lamb's bride was to be brought into existence and made a living reality. It was proper to characterize the Church as the wife, since she was married to Christ, and it was natural that spiritual children should be born of that union and into the family. Just as it was impossible for woman to have been created before the opening of Adam's side when that which formed her was taken out, even so it is equally impossible for the Church to have been brought into existence previous to the shedding of the blood of the Son of God.

But someone might say: "The Bible says that Christ loved the Church and gave himself for her, therefore it must have been in existence, or else he could not have given himself for her.

Well, it is true that Jesus had some followers, but they were not known or called his wife, and they did not become such until Christ died, made the sacrifice, and gave himself for them. Then they became his bride, or his wife. When a young man falls in love with a young lady, he is willing to forsake his father and mother and all things and give himself to her and for her, because he loves her. But was she his wife previous to the time that he gave himself for her? She was in existence as a young lady, but not as his wife, and she did not become a wife until he forsook all others, pledged his life, and gave himself for her. So it was with the Church of Christ. Human beings were in existence before they were known as a Church, but they were not in existence as a bride, or as the wife of Jesus, until he purchased them and the marriage was consummated. Then they are joined unto him as a bride, over which he becomes the head, and in which his Spirit dwells, and they blend into one.

Paul said, in **Rom.7:1-4**, "Know you not, brethren, (for I speak to them that know the law) how that the law has dominion over a man as long as he lives? For the woman that has a husband is bound by the law to her husband as long as he lives; but if the husband be dead, she is loosed from the law of her husband. So then if, while her husband lives, she be married to another man, she shall be called an adulteress: but if her husband be dead, she is free from that law; so that she is no adulteress, though she be married to another man. Wherefore, my brethren, you also are become dead to the law by the body of Christ; that you should be married to another, even to him who is raised from the dead, that we should bring forth fruit unto God."

What is Paul talking about? So long as the Law of Moses was in existence, the Israelites were married to that law as their husband. If during its effectiveness, they had been married to another law, they would have been guilty of spiritual adultery, but if the 'first law was blotted out, then they are loosed from it, and are not adulterers, though they be married to another law, or another man. Paul said: "You brethren are become dead to the law by the body of Christ that you should be married to another."

What other? Unto him. What him? Unto him who is raised from the dead. Not the one who walked over the hills of Judea, and the plains of Samaria in his personal ministry – not married unto him until he tasted death, but married unto him that is raised from the dead. The man does not live who can find the marriage consummated between Christ and the Church previous to the resurrection of the Son of God from the dead.

But what is the object of this marriage, Paul? "That ye should be married to another, even to him who is raised from the dead, that we should bring forth fruit unto God."

Now when he says fruit here, we do not understand it to mean the good works, which are to result from our union with Christ, but men and women born as the result of the marriage of Christ and the Church. Let me point out that the children born outside of that wedlock and relationship would be illegal in their state.

We said all of that in order to say this: The Church, having become married to Christ, has the right to take upon itself the name of the husband, and the children that will result from that union, have the right to take the name of the husband or the head of the household, and become members of the family of God. They will also become heirs of all that Jesus has, because they are born into the family of God, and are therefore heirs of God, and joint-heirs, with Jesus Christ.

Since the Church is described as the bride of Christ, doesn't it seem to you that the Church should wear his name? Does it seem reasonable that Jesus would come to earth, sorrow, suffer, bleed and die to establish the Church, and then the Church would dishonor Christ by refusing to wear his name, but would instead wear the name of some man? Also, we can see that since Jesus shed his blood to purchase the Church, (Acts.20:28) that if we are saved by his blood, we must be in the Church.

Is the Church essential to salvation? In reply to that question, I ask: Is Jesus' blood essential to salvation? Remember, he purchased the Church with his blood. If he gave his blood for the Church, and it is only by the blood that we can be saved, then it would seem that the Church should be worth what Jesus paid for her.

If I paid 100 dollars for a suit of clothes, the only way I would get any benefit out of the 100 dollars that I paid would be to wear the suit of clothes. In the same way, Jesus gave himself for the Church, (Eph.5:25) and purchased her with his blood, (Acts.20:28) therefore I must be in the Church to receive any benefit from his purchase price.

We may see how Jesus looks at the Church from another thought in the New Testament. In Acts.8:3, it is said that Saul made havoc of the Church. But in Acts.9:4, Jesus asked Saul: "Why persecute you me?" Therefore, to persecute the Church is to persecute Christ. I do not believe people can honor Christ and glorify him, and at the same time downgrade and belittle the bride of Christ, which is the Church.

The Bible says that Christ is the head of the Church, (Eph.5:23) and in Col.1:18, and Col.1:24, that the body of Christ is the Church. To separate the head from the body would be to destroy both. That proves that the Church is essential.

Sometimes people say: "Oh, I don't believe the Church is essential to salvation." Let me ask: Do you believe that Jesus would be the head of something that is non-essential? And the Bible also states that Christ is the Savior of the body. (Eph.5:23) If you think that the Church is non-essential, you will have to get another Savior, for Christ is said to be the Savior of the body over which he rules as head, that is, the Church. Are you a member of the Church that Jesus built? (Matt.16:18)

Chapter Two

THIRTEEN APOSTLES & WHAT BECAME OF THEM

CREDOHOUSEMINISTRY
By Permission

Christ did not shed His blood for the Church to live a life of ease, luxury and affluence, but one of Spirit power, righteousness, peace, joy and dominion over the reigns and regime of darkness.

He lived His life in keeping with the will of God, His Father, in the face and presence of the world. He died as a **Martyr**, giving us an example that we should follow, not just for the first century saints, but for all of His saints, till He comes again to take them home. Every saint that had his or her life cut short of living it out for a full day, (that is 1000 years) will come back again, and live out a full day, and makes 1000 years like Jesus Christ. (Rev.20:4)

In today's world, the majority of the saints of Christ are living a life of ease, affluence and luxury in Zion, but none of the first century apostles and believers ever lived like that. They followed the examples of their Lord and Savior, Jesus Christ. They could, but the urgency of the Lord's command compelled them to live a different life. Almost all of the first century believers died as martyrs, especially the Apostles of Christ. In the following pages, the author has included the lives of the Apostles, and the way they died, obeying the commands of their Lord, and paying for, and sowing the Gospel with their blood and lives. The orders of things changed from the second century onward with the Church Fathers as they introduced a different Gospel, making it an organization, and a movement of man, thus beginning an era where the Church is now called an organization or denomination today. They called themselves Bishops, Church Fathers, Pope and all kinds of honorific titles.

Martyrdom has always been common with God's people. Part of humanity who is opposed to and hated God, persecuted the righteous. We can trace this back to when mankind first began, when Cain slew his brother Abel, because God accepted his brother's sacrifice, and rejected his. Joseph, who was sold into slavery by his brothers, because he shared his dream from God, and that he was to be exalted above his brothers. Many of these stories are typology of what happened to Christ. Jesus warned that if they hated him, they would also hate us who follow him. (Lk.23:31) One of the blessings in the Scripture is upon those who are persecuted for His namesake. Peter says the glory of God rests on such people that are so persecuted for righteousness sake. (1Pet.4:13-19)

Heb.11:33-40: "Those who through faith subdued kingdoms, worked righteousness, obtained promises, stopped the mouths of lions, quenched the violence of fire, escaped the edge of the sword, out of weakness were made strong, became valiant in battle, and turned to flight the armies of the aliens. Women received their dead raised to life again. And others were tortured, not accepting deliverance, that they might obtain a better resurrection. Still others had trial of mockings and scourgings, yes, and of chains and imprisonment. They were stoned, sawn in two, tempted, and slain with the sword. They wandered about in sheepskins and goatskins, being destitute, afflicted, tormented; of whom the world was not worthy.

They wandered in deserts and mountains, in dens and caves of the earth. And all these, having obtained a good testimony through faith, did not receive the promise, God having provided something better for us; that they should not be made perfect apart from us. The resurrection was what the whole Church and saints of the Old Testament will share together. They were being persecuted because of their commitment, and this was not foreign to the saints. It was a normal way of life for the Old Testament prophets and the saints.

In Matt.23, Jesus rebuked the religious leaders of his day with seven woes, and then made this assessment in vv.34-35: "Therefore, indeed, I send you prophets, wise men and scribes: some of them you will kill and crucify, and some of them, you will scourge in your synagogues, and persecute from city to city, "that on you may come all the righteous blood shed on the earth, from the blood of righteous Abel, to the blood of Zechariah, son of Berechiah, whom you murdered between the temple and the altar." They intentionally rejected the righteous, just as their forefathers did. So, Jesus Christ attributes the guilt of all those who murdered the righteous and the prophets on them. Why was the sentence so great? Because they had One before them who is greater than all the prophets, and saw the greatest amount of miracles, and despite all the signs given, they still stayed in unbelief.

In Mk.12:1-12, Jesus gave a parable teaching that God sent many servants to his vineyard, (Israel) but they ended up killing them, until finally, He sent His Son. (vv.6-7; Lk.20:13-15) The story illustrates how the prophets were sent to their own people, who rejected and killed them. The promise at the end of the story was that the Vineyard would be put into the hand of the Church to cultivate. However, what Israel did to their prophets, would be done to the Church. After Israel was scattered, Rome would do the same, and eventually, the political Roman Church itself, would adopt its policy, centuries later for conversion.

Jesus warned those who followed him early on in Matt.10:17-21: "But beware of men, for they will deliver you up to councils and scourge you in their synagogues. You will be brought before governors and kings for My sake, as a testimony to them, and to the Gentiles. (v.21) Now, brother will deliver up brother to death, and a father his child; and children will rise up against parents and cause them to be put to death."

It was not an apostle who was the first martyr. It was Stephen. He was a deacon who became the first martyr, because he reminded the Pharisees of their fathers' rejection, in the wilderness, and Jesus' words in Matt.23. In one of the greatest and boldest sermons ever recorded in the Bible by the Spirit of God, Stephen states in Acts.7:52, "Which of the prophets did your fathers not persecute? And they killed those who foretold of the coming of the Just One, of whom you now have become the betrayers and murderers". Is it any wonder they killed him on the spot! We are told by Luke, "There arose a great persecution against the Church who was at Jerusalem;" and that "they were all scattered abroad throughout the regions of Judea and Samaria, except the apostles." It is said that about two thousand Christians suffered martyrdom during this time, as Acts.11:19 tells us, "Those who were scattered after the persecution that arose over Stephen, traveled as far as Phoenicia, Cyprus and Antioch."

Jesus Christ said we are to be witnesses of him to the ends of the earth. This also meant martyrdom, and in the beginning, no one understood the sacrifice of what this calling meant. In the time of the apostles, the term marturus was used in the sense of a witness, who at any time might be called upon to deny his testimony to Christ, by penalty of death.

To take up one's cross not only meant suffering, but could very well have meant death to the average believer. It did then, and it still does today. When Jesus said, "But you shall receive power when the Holy Spirit has come upon you; and you shall be witnesses to Me in Jerusalem, and in all Judea, and in Samaria, and to the end of the earth." (Acts.1:8) **They needed the power of God to sustain them, not only in their missionary work, but how their mission would end.**

Jesus prophesied to the Church in Matt.24:9; "Then they will deliver you up to tribulation, and kill you, and you will be hated by all nations for My name's sake." We are not to be loved and accepted by the world. If the world loves us, then, we are not loving God in the correct manner. Jesus said, "Woe to you when all men shall speak well of you, for so did their fathers to the false prophets." (Lk. 6:26)

During the persecutions in the early Church, many apostles became martyrs. James, the son of Zebedee was sawn asunder, and this was recorded in Acts.12:1-3. "Now about that time, Herod the king stretched out his hand to harass some from the Church. Then he killed James, the brother of John with the sword. And because he saw that it pleased the Jews, he proceeded further to seize Peter also." But it was not Peter's time as an angel rescued him, while the saints prayed. Both Peter and Paul were eventually martyred in Rome about 66 A.D., during the persecution under Emperor Nero. Paul was beheaded with the sword. Peter was crucified upside down at his request, since he did not feel he was worthy to die in the same manner as his Lord.

Andrew preached in Asia Minor, modern-day Turkey, and in Greece, and he was crucified on an "X"-shaped cross. It is known today as St. Andrew's Cross.

Philip had a far-reaching ministry in Carthage, North Africa, and in Asia Minor. He converted the wife of a Roman proconsul, who retaliated by having Philip arrested, scourged and thrown into prison. Afterwards, he was crucified at Heliopolis, in Phrygia, A. D. 54.

Simon, the Zealot was ministering in Persia, and was killed after refusing to sacrifice to the sun god. Mark was dragged on the ground, and his flesh fell to pieces. The people who were opposed to Christ in Alexandria were watching. According to Foxes Book of Martyrs, Matthias, who replaced Judas in the closed group of twelve apostles to Israel, was stoned at Jerusalem, and then beheaded.

James, who was the pastor of the Jerusalem Church; step brother of Jesus Christ, and author of the Epistle that bore his name, died in 62 A.D by his fellow brethren that he tried so desperately to reach. The Sanhedrin's Pharisees and Sadducees assembled, demanding him to declare from the galleries, that Jesus was not the Messiah. He went to the roof, and instead of blaspheming the name, he shouted out Jesus is the Son of God, and the judge of the world. The enraged Jews hurled him off the temple, and he was then beaten. As he was being stoned, he prayed as Jesus did, "Father forgive them, for they know not what they do." He finally had his life ended with a club.

This persecution continued in the early Church as the apostle Paul writes in 1Thess.2:14-15: "For you also suffered the same things from your own countrymen, just as they did from the Judeans, who killed both the Lord Jesus, and their own prophets, and have persecuted us; and they do not please God, and are contrary to all men." Although it was a Jewish Church in the beginning, most of the religious Jews opposed the gospel as Paul explains, "Concerning the gospel, they are enemies for your sake, but concerning the election, they are beloved for the sake of the fathers." (Rom.11:28)

Antipas, was a convert from paganism, and he was spoken of as a "faithful witness by Jesus, who wrote to the Church at Pergamos in Rev.2:13: "I know your works, and where you dwell, where Satan's throne is. And you hold fast to My name, and did not deny My faith, even in the days in which Antipas was My faithful martyr, who was killed among you, where Satan dwells."

There were known to be ten waves of persecutions under the Roman Emperors. Christians were tortured, even women, the young and old, whole families died for their faith in horrible ways. Drowning, burning parts of the body, being torn into pieces, burnings at the stake and being beheaded were commonplace. It is said for several weeks the countryside was lit up by Christians that were torched. **The amazing thing that happened which upset their tormentors was that the Christians were still smiling after their death.** But with all of these being done, the Church increased. No one could say anything against the brave faith illustrated by these martyrs facing death. God's grace was upon them, even more so in their death.

Some of the most vicious persecutions were under the watch of Emperor Trajan. Ignatius wrote before his exit, "Now I begin to be a disciple. I care for nothing, of visible or invisible things, so that I may, but win Christ. Let fire and the cross, let the companies of wild beasts, let breaking of bones and tearing of limbs, let the grinding of the whole body, and all the malice of the devil come upon me; be it so, only may I win Christ Jesus!" As he heard the lions roaring, he said. "I am the wheat of Christ: I am going to be ground with the teeth of wild beasts, that I may be found pure bread." (Foxes Book Martyrs)

Matt.5:43: "You have heard that it was said, "You shall love your neighbor and hate your enemy, but I say to you, love your enemies, bless those who curse you, do good to those who hate you, and pray for those who spitefully use you and persecute you, that you may be the sons of your Father in heaven; for He makes His sun rise on the evil and on the good." These men and many others lived out the command, even in their death.

Paul in giving his testimony to Agrippa, recalls his witnessing the first martyr. "So I said, 'Lord, they know that in every synagogue, I imprisoned and beat those who believe on You. And when the blood of Your martyr, Stephen was shed, I also was standing by, consenting to his death, and guarding the clothes of those who were killing him." (Acts.22:19-20) Certainly this became a seed of truth planted in Paul's life as he stood by, consenting with the others of Stephen's death.

Paul later echoed Jesus' sermon on the mount in Rom.12:14, "Bless those who persecute you; bless and do not curse." (Rom.12:20-21) "Therefore, if your enemy is hungry, feed him; if he is thirsty, give him a drink; for in so doing, you will heap coals of fire on his head. Do not be overcome by evil, but overcome evil with good." There was high visibility of love in the early Church, and it showed in the sacrifices they made as the apostle John wrote, **"By this we know love, because He laid down His life for us. And we also ought to lay down our lives for the brethren." (1Jn.3:16-17)**

It is from the writings of the Church Fathers that we know the history of the early Church. Clement and Eusibuis wrote of their history. This statement has echoed over the centuries of time "the seed of the Church is built on the blood of the martyrs." Death was such a common way to go that it was called the baptism of blood. Christians were called atheists because they would not recognize Caesar as God. They did not need to have him as their only God, but only add him to Jesus and they would be spared. Many did not compromise, yet some did. In the first few centuries there were six million martyrs.

As the early Church developed, so did their doctrines. While the apologists gave defense of Christ to the pagan world, challenges came from the inside of the Church that gave rise to Polemicists. Now the Church was in need of bulwarks to protect her from the inside, what was entrusted to them from the apostles' teachings. The last of the apostles were gone and the teachings that were oral when they were alive, were now written down. Circulation of the Gospels and Paul's epistles were necessary for the Churches survival, not only to edify, but to protect it. The first two hundred years after the apostles, were the most crucial time for laying the groundwork against all the heresies that would try to take root inside the fertile, yet fragile ground of the new, but growing Church.

There were certain men who stood out in history that helped preserve the scriptures and rejected the forgeries that many claimed had apostolic authority. It is a few of these certain men I will focus on that were bold speakers against the philosophies of their day, and stood firm against those from inside the Church that distorted the nature of God and Christ. These men were uncompromising, determined to continue in the truth, and gave their lives as a consequence as they were martyred for their beliefs.

Today we have many of their writings of which one could put together over ninety percent of the N.T. from their own penmanship. Rome had conquered the world and the Church was being persecuted at an enormous rate.

All of these martyrs lived one hundred years before the council of Nicea that was the first official council on doctrine. The Church then was no longer underground, but became an organization that became a detriment to its cause. Let us look at several of these heroes of the faith that defended the word and delivered the Scriptures to their country and us today. Theirs was a testimony of blood that was considered the greatest of honors. Like Stephen, who was the first to prove his inner strength of faith, he stood as a beacon to his brethren in the Church, and to the Pharisee's who killed him for his preaching and the testimony of Jesus Christ.

John the Apostle was the last to survive, being the only one to have died a natural death from old age. During Domitian's persecution in the middle of 90 A.D, he was banished to the

Isle of Patmos. Being exiled, he wrote the last book of the New Testament--the Revelation. It was John who wrote in Rev.12:11: "And they overcame him by the blood of the Lamb, and by the word of their testimony, and they did not love their lives unto death."

This was and still is, the approval of God's grace on every martyr for the Christian faith. Of the many disciples he made, one stands out who was called Polycarp, who lived from 69-155 A.D. The writings tell us that he was a disciple of Peter, Paul and John. He became the chief presbyter over the Church at Smyrna, and taught Irenaeus of Lyons, who was one of the greatest theologians we know of in his time. Irenaeus succeeded bishop Pothirus when he died in the persecutions. Irenaeus died in 190 A.D. (Rev.2:10)

When Polycarp was brought before the judge, and commanded to reject and blaspheme Christ, he decisively answered, "Eighty and six years have I served him, and he never did me wrong, how then can I blaspheme my King who has saved me?" It is written of Polycarp, "So it befell the blessed Polycarp, who having with those from Philadelphia suffered martyrdom in Smyrna--twelve in all--is especially remembered more than the others by all men, so that he is talked of even by the heathen in every place: for he showed himself not only a notable teacher, but also a distinguished martyr, whose martyrdom all desire to imitate, seeing that it was after the pattern of the Gospel of Christ."

"Fixing their minds on the grace of Christ, [the martyrs] despised worldly tortures, and purchased eternal life, but a single hour. To them, the fire of their cruel torturers was cold. They kept before their eyes their escape from the eternal and unquenchable fire." Polycarp joined six others who were scourged and beheaded. He was sentence to die by burning at the stake, by Antoninus Pius in the market place before a crowd.

Ignatius, who was a friend of Polycarp, became bishop at Antioch. He was fed to the lions at the Coliseum of Rome, under Trajan in 117 A.D.. Justin Martyr, an apologist for the faith, confronted Marcion, who rejected the Old Testament and issued his own New Testament, in which consisted part of the Gospel of Luke, and 10 of Paul's epistles only. He was so bold, he wrote a defense of Christianity, and addressed it to the Emperor. Augustus Caesar wrote, "You can kill us, but you cannot hurt us." Justin also died a martyr, beheaded at Rome in 67 A.D.. Origen, who seemed to waver between right doctrine of God's nature, and sometimes heresy in other areas, defended the Christian faith against the pagans in 250 A.D. He was put in chains and terribly tortured.

In 250 A.D., the cry was "Cyprian to the lions, Cyprian to the beasts." In 257 A.D, Cyprian was brought before the proconsul, who exiled him to a little city on the Lybian Sea. On the death of this proconsul, Aspasius Paturnus, had Cyprian returned to Carthage, but was soon seized, and carried before the new governor, who condemned him to be beheaded. He was sentence to be executed on the 14th of September 258 A.D.

It was most confusing and challenging when the persecutions broke out from within the Church's walls. It was later, when the Arians had gained full control that the former deacon, Athanasius came to the forefront to battle long and hard over their doctrine of Christ being a creature only, and not deity in man. Historian Philip Schaff comments on the Arian movement, stating, "Arianism was a religious political war against the spirit of the Christian revelation by the spirit of the world, which, after, having persecuted the Church three hundred years from without, sought under the Christian name to reduce her by degrading Christ to the category of the temporal and the created, and Christianity to the level of natural religion."

It became the issue in the Church, and for the next 50 years, Arianism became a major movement inside the Church from

Rome. There were many others who defended Christ as God and the doctrine of the triune nature, but did not have the privilege to give their lives, but continued to live for the truth. Athanasius defending the deity and tri-unity of God's nature was almost killed within the Church as disputes of doctrine became overheated.

In 353 A.D., Constantius, Constantine's son, became the ruler over the whole Empire. He was a pro Arian sympathizer like his father. In 356 A.D., Athanasius was attacked during his Church service by Arians, who brought along with him 5,000 Roman troops. He escaped with his life, and spent the next six years in exile with monks in the surrounding area. Athanasius was exiled over five times until the Arian influence finally disintegrated, and the controversy culminated at the Council of Constantinople in 381 A.D. The rift that divided the Church for fifty years would finally end.

Remember what Jesus said before Pilate, "If my kingdom were of this world, my followers would fight." The early Church did not take up the sword, but instead, laid down their lives. **It was not many centuries later, when a deceived Church wanted to take over the world religiously and politically. By doing this, they forfeited being the Church that Christ found. One is not to fight for their faith, when they are persecuted for it.**

The Scripture instructs the believers, "He that leads into captivity, shall go into captivity: he that kills with the sword, must be killed with the sword." The only time martyrs are mentioned specifically is in Rev.17:6, when John sees the counterfeit Church annihilating the saints, he writes: "I saw the woman, drunk with the blood of the saints and with the blood of the martyrs of Jesus. And when I saw her, I marveled with great amazement."

Tertullian stated, "No man would be willing to die unless he knew he had the truth." In countries that are communist,

Muslim and anti Christian, there are many that face the same choice, and the early Church did. Reject Jesus, or die. There are those being persecuted, who experientially know the meaning of carrying their cross. Here in America, we give some of our money and a little of our time, and feel we have done our duty. This is incomparable to those who give their lives. In 1997-98 in about 60 different countries, there were 160,000 Christians each year that we know of, who gave their lives for the faith. That is approximately 450 a day. The highest percentage comes from Islamic fundamentalists. Persecution of Christians continues on the upswing, and the Gospel may soon be considered a hate crime. Imagine the very thing that shows the Love of God for the people of the world will soon be silenced in the name of peace and unity for mankind.

"Precious in the sight of the Lord is the death of His saints." (Psm.116:15) We need to remember our brethren in our prayers. In Jn.15, Jesus tells the apostle how he has chosen them for their mission, and that they are no longer part of the world and its kingdom, but are now of God's kingdom. In vs.20, "Remember the word that I said to you, 'A servant is not greater than his master.' If they persecuted Me, they will also persecute you. If they kept My word, they will keep yours also."

We are to be salt and light in a corrupting world. We are to be an influence on the world, not the world influencing us. We are to stand against and hold back the corrupting influence of sin and sinners who want to influence others, especially the young. We are in the world, but separated for service to Christ. When we stand up for righteousness that is found in Christ and God's word, we should expect people to be against us. But it is not us they are really against, but God's standards and principles.

Jesus said about the end of time before his return, when all the things are in place, "But before all these things, they will lay their hands on you and persecute you, delivering you up to the assemblies and prisons. You will be brought before kings and rulers for My name's sake." (Lk.21:12)

It is first the saints in the tribulation that are persecuted and killed as John witnesses the fifth seal being opened, "I saw under the altar the souls of those who had been slain for the word of God and for the testimony which they held." (Rev.6:9) They were given white robes waiting for the full number of the brethren to be killed as they were. (Rev.7) As they are finished being persecuted by Satan, God begins sealing 144,000 Jewish believers to be even greater witnesses. It is then that Satan turns to Israel, who will be his target of persecuted for the last three and half years.

I don't believe that the Bible teaches the Church will go through the great tribulation, however, much of the Church, throughout the world, has already been under great persecution much like the early Church. While we are not experiencing a physical persecution here in America yet, (except for a few instances) should we be so comfortable in saying that it cannot happen here in America as in other countries?

Today in America and other prosperous countries, we are left hardly knowing the truth despite all the "Christian Programming" on TV. Many want to Christianize the world, and it probably won't be long before we make the same mistakes of abandoning the power of the Gospel and showing the light of Christ in us instead, and want to use force to convert others. Any religion that uses force shows that it is weak in convincing people, that it has something from God. Using force to enforce ones religion, (Christian or not) proves they do not represent the true God.

Because of pressure from the world and other religions, we are unwilling to speak out against those who misrepresent Christ or hate Him. Tolerance is rotting our witness in society. Unlike the early Church, they grew from contending openly for the faith, and they grew from contention. Few do this any longer, and would certainly be unwilling to die for him if it became necessary. It has become the silence of the Lambs. The path of least resistance is chosen, and we have in some ways become as tolerant as some liberals. We may one day soon need to have the courage the first century Church had or go out with a whimper.

HOW THEY DIED

I have an interest in the death of the Apostles. We all should. Every Christian should spend some time looking into the historical records. There are many legends concerning their death that make the historical evidence hard to interpret. Many times the accounts conflict with one another. Most early Christians wanted their home to be crowned with the stature of having been the final resting place of one of the twelve. It is probably for this reason that there were embellishments forged.

Sifting through the wheat and the chaff is not easy task. The martyrdom of some of the Apostles is more certain than others. Historians will have different degrees of certainty concerning the circumstances of their deaths. For instance, unbiased historians will not take issue with the historical credibility of the martyrdom of Peter, Paul, and James and the apostle. Many of the other accounts have recent historic validity as well. Some accounts, however, raise the eyebrow and cause us to remain agnostic.

However, when boiled down to their least common denominator, it is very feasible to believe that all, but one of the apostles suffered and died a martyr's death, even if we can't be sure of the exact details.

Amidst some uncertainty, one thing is clear—the reason given for their death was the same in all accounts. They were killed because they proclaimed to have seen Christ die, and then to have seen Him alive. They all died because of an unwavering, unrelenting claim that Christ rose from the grave. They died for the Passover.

Personally, in my mind, the gruesome death of the apostles as recorded below was one of the greatest gifts that God ever gave to the Church. It contributes much to Christian apologetics by answering the "how do you know?" question concerning the resurrection of Christ.

The following is my attempt to take the best of all the sources, and share the most likely scenario for each apostle's death. At the risk of spoiling some of the "legends,"

Read through the accounts of their deaths. Use it this Passover. Tell your children. This may sound odd, but in a very real sense, I thank God for bringing about the apostles' deaths, for in their deaths, they sealed their testimony in blood, making our faith in the risen Christ, built upon a solid foundation.

HOW THEY PERFORMED

"Go yea into all the world and preach the good news to every creature." SO THEY DID. But where did they go? What did they do? And what happened to them? Let us use Da Vinci's "Last Supper"

Bartholomew: He was skinned alive and beheaded. Preached the Gospel in Mesopotamia (Iraq), Persia (Iran), Turkey, Armenia and India. He was killed at Derbent, Azerbaijan, near Russia on the Caspian Sea by order of a local king, after a majority of the people of Derbent converted to Christianity. Some of Bartholomew's skin and bones are still kept in The Basilica of St. Bartholomew in Rome, a part of his skull is in

Frankfurt, Germany and an arm is venerated at the Canterbury Cathedral in England.

James, the Lesser: He was stoned and clubbed to-death. Believed to have preached in Damascus, (Syria) and acknowledged as the first bishop of the Christians in Jerusalem, Israel. Historians say that he was sentenced to be stoned to death by the Jews for challenging Jewish Laws, and for convincing some of the members of the Jewish community to convert to Christianity. James died during the stoning, and one the people from the crowd approached him, and bashed his head with a fullers club, a piece of wood used for bashing-washing clothes. He was buried on the spot where he died, somewhere in Jerusalem.

Andrew: He was crucified upside down on an X-shaped cross. Preached in Georgia, (Russia) Istanbul (Turkey), Macedonia and finally Greece. There in Patros, Greece, the governor, Aegiatis, was angered by the apostle's preaching, and the conversion of his own family to Christianity. He ordered Andrew to renounce his faith in front of a tribunal. When Andrew resisted, the governor ordered that Andrew be crucified. He was tied upside down to an X-shaped cross with thick, tight ropes, but Andrew kept preaching to spectators. He was able to convince many to accept Christianity just before he died, after suffering for three days. Parts of his remains are in Constantinople (Turkey), Scotland (England), but his skull is kept in Patras to this day.

Judas Iscariot: He committed suicide by hanging. Best known as the apostle who betrayed the Lord by divulging His location, leading to His arrest and eventual death. He received 30 pieces of silver from the Jewish priests for the information he gave. Prior to this, Judas served as the treasurer of the 12 Apostles, in charge of keeping the group's money. Sources could not agree on how he died. There are three accepted versions: (1) He committed suicide by hanging himself to a tree. (2) He accidentally fell on a field– head first. (3) He was crushed by a passing chariot. (4) He was stoned to death by the other 11

Apostles. But all four agreed that "his bowels gushed out" on all four accounts. Authors and scholars also agree that his guilt was a major part of the cause of his death. The Scripture tells us that he committed suicide. (Acts.1:17-20)

Peter: He was crucified upside down. Recognized as the head of the original Christian community in Jerusalem, Israel. He left the city when king Herod Agrippa I started to persecute all Christians in Jerusalem, and ordered the beheading of the Apostle James, the Great. After escaping from Jerusalem, Peter preached in Judea, originally Palestine, and in Antioch, Syria, where he is historically considered as the first patriarch bishop of the Orthodox Church.

After staying in Antioch for some time, Peter went to Rome, and converted thousands into Christianity. The Emperor at the time, Nero, did not like the idea of Romans becoming Christians, and used the new members of the group for his amusement. For an example, he fed them to lions or wild dogs, and then burnt them at stake in Rome's coliseum. Yes, the tourist spot– if they do not renounce their faith. Peter was one of the most prominent victims of this persecution. He was captured and crucified upside down at his own request, because he said he was not worthy to be crucified the same way as our Lord. St. Peter's body lies below the altar of St. Peter's Basilica at the Vatican City, in Rome.

John: He was thrown into boiling oil, but survived. For most of his labors, John was with Peter in Jerusalem up until the persecution of Herod Agrippa I. During this period, scholars agree that John escaped and preached for sometime in Asia Minor, an area around Turkey. Years later, scholars have traced that he went to Rome where it was believed he was persecuted with other Christians, and was thrown into a cauldron of boiling oil. He miraculously survived. The Roman Emperor Domitian at the time, decided after the incident to banish John to the island of Patmos in Greece. When Domitian died, John went back to Ephesus in Turkey, where he spent the rest of his days. He died a very old man, the only Apostle to do so.

Thomas: He was impaled by a spear. Called by most Christians as the "Doubting Thomas" for disbelieving the Lord's Resurrection. But after his doubts were erased by touching Jesus' wounds, he became a fearless preacher of the Gospel and builder of Church. He was the only Apostle who witnessed the Assumption of Mary, and the one of the first Apostles who preached outside the boundaries of the vast Roman Empire out of Europe. He preached in Babylon, present day Iraq, and established its first Christian Church. Then he went to Persia in Iran, and travelled as far as China and India. He was martyred in Mylapore, India, when a local king named Masdai condemned him to death. The Apostle angered the Brahmins, high ranked priests/scholars who served as the king's advisers, and thought Christianity disrespected India's Caste System. Thomas was brought to a nearby mountain and was stabbed to death with a spear. He was believed to have been buried around the suburb of Madras, in India.

James: He was beheaded by Herod, the great. He was the brother of the Apostle John. He decided to preached the Gospel in Iberia around Spain, and be the first to build a Christian Foundation in the area. But according to some scholars, the Virgin Mary appeared to James and told him to return to Judea to help the other Apostles. He was captured and condemned to die by Herod Agrippa 1 to please Jewish leaders who were furious at the rapid growth of the Church. James' chief accuser was later convinced that the Apostle was indeed blessed by the Lord. He himself requested to be beheaded with James. After this, James' body was brought back to Spain by his disciples, and was buried in the area where the cathedral of Santiago de Compostela is located, which is now considered as a major religious site.

Phillip: He preached in Greece, Syria and Turkey, and in the cities of Galatia, Phrygia and Hierapolis. Philip partnered with Bartholomew in his missions. Like all Apostles, Philip became an exceptional speaker. According to sources, "Through his miraculous healing and preaching, Philip converted the wife of the Proconsul of the city" of Hierapolis. Of course, this event angered the Proconsul, and he ordered that both Philip and Bartholomew be tortured and crucified upside down. While on the cross, Philip continued to preach, and he was able to convince the crowd and the Proconsul to release Bartholomew, while insisting that he remained crucified. Bartholomew was released, but Philip died on the cross, and was later buried somewhere within the city.

Matthew: He was burned to death. He was a rich tax collector and the most educated among the Apostles. Christian tradition says he preached in Ethiopia, Judea, Macedonia, Syria and Parthia, Northeast Iran. Bible scholars have different versions on how he died. Some say he was either killed with a sword in Parthia, or he died a natural death in Ethiopia. The most interesting and dramatic story appeared here, where it says Matthew came to a city, and was able to convert the family of the local king to Christianity.

This angered the king and ordered his soldiers to capture Matthew. In front of a huge crowd, they nailed him unto a bed, covered his whole body with paper, oil, brimstone, asphalt, brushwood, and then they set him ablaze. Matthew was able to endure the torture while praising and preaching, but eventually died "a happy death". Everyone who touched the burnt bed after, was miraculously healed, and converted into Christianity, including the king who asked for forgiveness, and became a staunch Christian believer.

Jude Thaddeus: He was axed to death. He was the Patron Saint of Desperate Cases and Lost Causes and a farmer, before becoming an apostle. He was a partner of Simon, the Zealot and together they preached and converted non-believers in Judea, Persia (Iran), Samaria (Israel), Idumaea (near Jordan), Syria, Mesopotamia (Iran) and Libya. It is also widely believed that Jude travelled and preached in Beirut, Lebanon. He also helped Bartholomew in bringing Christianity to Armenia. The cause of his death in unclear, because of the existence of two versions: (1) He was crucified in Edessa, Turkey. (2) He was clubbed to death, or his body was either sawed or axed in pieces after, together with Simon, the Zealot. Some sources say he was buried either in Northern Persia, or the most accepted version that his remains are buried in a crypt at St. Peter's Basilica in Rome.

Simon the Zealot: He was sawed or axed to death. Before becoming an apostle, Simon was a member of the "Zealots", a political movement rebelling against the Roman occupation of Jerusalem. Identified by some as the second Bishop of Jerusalem, after James, the Lesser who was beheaded. He is also believed to have preached in the Middle East, North Africa, Egypt, Mauritania and even Britain.

Paul, a persecutor of the Christian faith, (Gal.1:13) was brought to repentance on his way to Damascus by an appearance of the risen Christ. Ironically, Paul was heading for Damascus to arrest those who held to Christ's resurrection. Paul was the greatest skeptic there was, until he saw the truth of the resurrection. He then devoted his life to the proclamation of the living Christ. Writing to the Corinthians, defending his ministry, Paul tells of his sufferings for the name of Christ: "In labors more abundant, in beatings above measure, in prisons more frequent, in deaths often. Of the Jews five times received I forty stripes minus one.

Three times I was beaten with rods, once was I stoned, three times I suffered shipwreck, a night and a day, I have been in the deep; in journeys often, in storms on the water, in danger of robbers, in danger by mine own countrymen, in danger by the heathen, in danger in the city, in danger in the wilderness, in the sea, among false brethren; in weariness and painfulness, in watchings often, in hunger and thirst, in fastings often, in cold and nakedness." (2Cor.11:23-27) Finally, Paul met his death at the hands of the Roman Emperor Nero, when he was beheaded in Rome. Date of Martyrdom 67 A.D.

THE NEW TESTAMENT REALITY

At Pentecost, fifty days after the resurrection of the Lord Jesus Christ, God did a remarkable thing. He set aside the Temple, the old building made with human hands, along with the entire legal systems that represented it. He replaced it with a new Spiritual Temple. This new Temple was not made of bricks, stones, nails, wood and other materials, but people who are washed in the blood of Christ, the Son of the Living God. He then relocated the expression of His glory in the redeemed, by His Spirit.

And what agreement hath the temple of God with idols? For you are the temple of the living God; as God has said, I will dwell in them, and walk in *them*; and I will be their God, and they shall be my people. (2Cor.6:16) Know you not that you are the Temple of God, and *that* the Spirit of God dwells in you? (1Cor.3:16)

Now therefore you are no more strangers and foreigners, but fellow citizens with the saints, and of the Household of God. And are built upon the foundation of the apostles and prophets, Jesus Christ Himself being the Chief Corner Stone. In whom all the building fitly framed together grows unto a holy Temple in the Lord. In whom you also are built together for a habitation of God through the Spirit. (Eph.2:19-22)

The spiritual building is made up of both Jewish and Gentile Christians who are placed together into a living Organism, built of Living Stones that pulsate with the very Life of God. And the Scripture says, "You also, as living stones, are built up a Spiritual House, a Holy Priesthood to offer up spiritual sacrifices to God through Jesus Christ." (1Pet.2:5) The Church as a whole is represented by "You" and designated as a chosen generation, a royal priesthood, a holy nation, a peculiar people that should show forth the praises of Him who has called you (Church) out of darkness into His marvelous light. (1Pet.2:9)

Today our invisible God locates Himself not in physical buildings, but in those people who belong to Him, and have passed through the blood of Christ. The bodies of believers have become the dwelling place of God, which is the body of Christ. Believers, not buildings, are the Church. Believers are the House of God, called the Church on earth. We are the members of His body, of His flesh, and of His bones. This is a great mystery: but I speak concerning Christ and the Church. (Eph.5:30, 32)

Chapter Three

I AM OF THE CHURCH

(IN CHRIST)
(I AM HIS REPLICA)

1. I am who God says I am
2. I am the salt of the earth. Matt.5:13
3. I am the light of the world. Matt.5:14
4. I am a child of God. Jn.1:12
5. I am a part of the true Vine. Jn.15:2
6. I am a channel of Christ's Life. Jn.15:1, 5
7. I am Christ's Friend. Jn.15:15
8. I am chosen in Christ.
9. I am appointed by Christ to bear His fruit. Jn.15:16
10. I am a slave of righteousness. Rom.6:18
11. I am enslaved to God. Rom.6:22
12. I am a son of God. Gal.3:26, 4:6 and Rom.8:14-15
13. I am a joint heir with Christ. Rom.8:17
14. I am a temple of God. 1Cor.3:16; 6:19
15. I am a member of Christ's body. 1Cor.12:27; Eph.5:30
16. I am united to the Lord.
17. I am one with the Jesus Christ. 1Cor.6:17, Gal.3:26, 28

18. I am a new creation. 2Cor.5:17
19. I am reconciled to God.
20. I am a minister of reconciliation. 2Cor.5:18-19
21. I am crucified with Christ. Gal.2:20
22. I am an heir of God. Gal.4:6-7
23. I am a saint. Eph.1:1; 1Cor.1:2
24. I am Christ's ambassador.
25. I am God's workmanship.
26. I am God's handiwork.
27. I am born anew in Christ to do His work. Eph.2:10
28. I am a fellow citizen with the saints. (God's Family) Eph.2:19
29. I am a prisoner of Christ. Eph.3:1; 4:1.
30. I am righteous and holy. Eph.4:24
31. I am a citizen of heaven. Phil.3:20, 2:6
32. I am seated in heaven right now.
33. I am hidden with Christ in God. Col.3:3.
34. I am an expression of the life of Christ. He is my life. Col.3:4
35. I am chosen of God, holy and dearly beloved. Col.3:12; 1Thes.1:4
36. I am a son of light and not of darkness. 1Thes.5:5
37. I am a holy partaker of a heavenly calling. Heb.3:1
38. I am a partaker of Christ. I share in His Life. Heb.3:14
39. I am one of God's living stones. 1Pet.2:5
40. I am being built up in Christ as a spiritual house. 1Pet.2:5
41. I am a member of a chosen race, a royal priesthood, a holy nation, a people for God's own possession. 1Pet.2:9, 10.
42. I am an alien and stranger to this world in which I temporarily live. 1Pet.2:11.
43. I am an enemy of the devil. 1Pet.5:8

44. I am a child of God, and I resemble Christ right now, and hereafter. 1Jn.3:1-2.
45. I am born of God, and the evil one, the devil, cannot touch me. 1Jn.5:18.
46. I am justified, forgiven and made righteous. Rom.5:1.
47. I am alive in Christ, and I am dead to the power of sin's rule over my life. Rom.6:1-6.
48. I am free forever from condemnation. Rom.8:1.
49. I am placed into Christ by God's doing. 1Cor.1:30.
50. I am in possession of the Spirit of God in my life that I might know the things that are freely given to me by God. 1Cor.2:12.
51. I am in possession of the mind of Christ. 1Cor.2:16.
52. I am bought with a price; I am not my own; I belong to God. 1Cor.6:19-20.
53. I am established, anointed, and sealed by God in Christ. God has given me His Spirit as a pledge, guaranteeing my inheritance to come. 1Cor.1:21; Eph.1:13-14.
54. I am living for Christ. 2Cor.5:14-15
55. I am made righteous in Christ. 2Cor.5:21
56. I am blessed with every spiritual blessing. Eph.1:3
57. I am chosen in Christ before the foundation of the world. Eph.1:4.
58. I am holy and blameless before God. Eph.1:4.
59. I am redeemed and forgiven. I am a recipient of God's lavish grace. Eph.1:6-8.
60. I am alive in Christ. Eph.2:5.
61. I am risen and seated with Christ in heaven. Eph.2:6.
62. I am given access to God's throne through the Spirit by Christ. Eph.2:18.

63. I am confident, and I do approach God with boldness and freedom. Eph.3:12.
64. I am transferred to the Kingdom of Christ, and I have been rescued from the domain of Satan's rule. Col.1:13.
65. I am redeemed and forgiven of all my sins. Col.1:14.
66. I am in Christ, and He is in me. Col.1:27.
67. I am firmly rooted in Christ, and I am being built up in Him. Col.2:7.
68. I am complete in Christ. Col.2:10.
69. I am buried with Christ, raised up in Him, and my life is now hidden with Christ in God. Christ is my life. Col.3:1-4.
70. I am in possession of the Spirit of power, love and self-discipline. 2Tim.1:7.
71. I am saved and set apart according to God's doing. 2Tim.1:9, Titus.3:5.
72. I am sanctified, and I am one with the Sanctifier. He is not ashamed to call me His brother / sister. Heb.2:11.
73. I am God's son / daughter, therefore, I have the right to come boldly before the throne of God to receive mercy, and find grace to help in time of need. Heb.4:16.
74. I am a partaker of His divine nature, therefore, I have been given precious and magnificent promises by God. 2Pet.1:4.
75. I am a replica of God, and He lives in me. Gen.2:7
76. I have angels with me, given by my Father, and always around. Psm.23:6; Heb.1:7, 14; Matt.18:10; Psm.34:7

Chapter Four

WITH YOU, IT SHALL NOT BE SO.

LK.22:25-30
(A WORD FROM THE LORD)

Is the Church that Christ is building, both an organism and organization? What kind of an organization is Christ building, and what are the materials that He uses in the construction of this organization?

There are those who believe amongst the saints of God, that the Church is both an organism and organization, and they gave their reasons for it being so.

They maintained that due to the growth and the progression of revelation, concept development was necessary to go forward. They said, those who have read that the NT Church met in homes, drew a conclusion that the Church should continually meet in homes. That it was out of necessity that the early Church met in homes. The arguments that the proponents of the Church as an organization made was that the Roman Government refused the followers of Christ, a sect of Judaism, to get permission to build a place of worship.

The Epistles are written for the purposes of organizing the Church, both for the preservation of sound doctrines, and the conduct of government. They said that the first period in history was over. Christianity was established in many cities, nations and empires. The existing Churches had grown enormously since the writing of the epistles of Paul and the apostles. That in Ephesus, the Church had grown into the community of very considerable size.

The argument went on to further say that the increase in numbers brought with it certain disadvantages and needs. One disadvantage was the impossibility of intimate personal acquaintance of all members of the Church with the apostles.

A Rebuttal: The Scriptures told us that God is omniscient, omnipotent and omnipresent. He knows every thing in this life, and has the knowledge of the 7.2 billion people who made up humanity at the present time. There is nothing hidden from Him. The Psalmist said, "The earth is the Lord's and the fullness thereof, and all that dwell on it…" (Psm.24:1-2; 89:11)

He knew all that would happen before Christ came to the earth. He knows all that happened when Christ was on the earth, and what will happen on earth at the end of the world. When Christ came to our planet, He declared that His Father had sent Him to procure and usher in redemption for humanity through His life, blood, death and resurrection from the dead. His blood was given for the lives of humanity, who will believe in His mission given by His Father.

Christ did not build a cathedral on earth for those who believed in Him. He had a complete knowledge of humanity, and what will happen in thousand years after He had returned to the right hand of the Father in heaven. As He carried out His mission that has been given to Him by His Father, the Church He has come to build grew, and He did not have mega building to contain her. His focus was on humanity, and not building, as His disciples watched Him in His mission. As thousands and thousands of mankind committed their lives to Christ, where to meet was not an issue at all. They met in homes, town halls, large buildings and wherever they found places to house His saints. He is quite capable and full of wisdom and knowledge in shepherding and housing His people, without mega structures. The idea of the Church becoming an organization was a mistake on the earth, by the people of God.

In Acts, the Church grew from addition to multiplication, and to number thousands of thousands of people. The intension of God was to dominate each city by having groups of 8-20 filling each Church of each city. In a city that has over 30,000 to 30 million people, He wants His Church to be in homes, houses and places that will house the saints in millions and millions of House Churches. He wanted them to function like this to avoid super ministers in both men and women.

There would be leaders and in a pluralistic manner, in whose lives Christ will be honored and seen as their King. The leadership knows its Lord, and these saints will not lord it over the people of God. They will not seek for honor, prestige, fame, power, glory and popularity. Jesus Christ had His fellowship of men and women who followed Him everywhere He went, and their number did not exceed twenty. He also had other seventy disciples and these ones also met for fellowship. He was the Leader of His entourage.

Today, He still wants to be the Boss of His Church, and He has set apostles, prophets, teachers, evangelist and pastors to serve amongst them as He served in the days of His flesh. (Eph.4:7-11, and 2:19-20) Instead of having mega building of 30,000 saints meeting in a single man-made structure, the Church can be spread out to over 3-20 thousand House Churches of 10-15 in a home. It will be better for the saints to divide into these House Churches, and serve the community of the saved and unsaved in the city.

Human will say that this is impossible, but there is nothing impossible or too hard for the Lord our God to perform. Things that are impossible to men, are possible to God. For an example, there are about 1.5 million people in the city of Winnipeg, and it has about 2-3 hundred denominational fellowships, meeting in their denominations with designated names, and their building, they called churches. If the Churches in Winnipeg had gone to House Churches, without taking on denominational names, the House Churches could be number in the thousands. It would have been up to 10,000-50,000 house fellowships in the city. There will be no names and any notable leader, except her Lord and Master, Jesus Christ who was a servant Leader and the Owner of the Church. Imagine the cities and the world filled with millions and billions of House Churches bearing no names, except for the cities, and the name of Jesus Christ, her Lord and Master!

Christendom could not believe that God would do it, and the saints who are hungry for power, prestige, domination, popularity, fame and all kinds of accolades moved from what it was to the present day denominational church movements. Now in the 21st century, we have super structures and mega churches who are ruled by larger than life personalities, and they called themselves the ministers of God. Think of the early disciples and the apostles of the Lord. How did they live and die?

These larger than life personalities will not want these House Churches, because of power, fame, wealth, riches, glory, prestige, honor and dominion over their fellow saints, rather than Christ being the Lord and Owner of His Church. Mankind loves titles, honors, authority and dominion over their kind. Therefore, we have names like reverends, apostles, arch-apostles, archbishops, bishops, archdeacons, deacons, doctor-reverends, prophets, teachers, evangelists, pastors and many others. There are offices that bore the consent of the Lord, and they are apostles, prophets, teachers, evangelists and pastors. These are the only titles and honor accepted by the Lord and the Church.

Those who argue that the Church is both an organism and organization need to revisit Matt.16:18. Jesus Christ said, "I will build My Church, and the gates (leaderships, authorities and powers) of hell will not overpower, nor prevail against her." Man-made buildings can be overpowered by the elements like fire, wind, blizzard, storms, rushing waters and satanically organized humanity, who opposes Christ and His Church. The Muslims are doing just that in the 21st century. They are pillaging, desecrating and destroying both physical structures and the saints of the Lord. It is imperative to know that the Church, who is a part and parcel of Christ, cannot be overcome, nor overpowered by man-made governments, or the power and the forces of hell, even Satan himself.

We have confused the Church that Christ is building with the one mankind is building. Certainly, the man-made church is subjected to all kinds of predators and enemies, and should be rightly called an organization. But we must never call the Church, who is in the image and likeness of Christ, an organization or a physical building. She is a being, an organism, and she can empathize, love, be joyful, peaceful, righteous, sad and capable of all kinds of emotions, positive and negative.

These ministers of God who want fame, popularity, power, importance, significance and the clout over other saints, seek to call the Church an organization. They have organized these churches by themselves, and they should be called organizations, instead of an organism. These ones are the heads of these organizations, and the brain behind their day-to-day existence, instead of Christ, the builder of His Church. These ones are the owners of the super church organizations, the mega cathedrals and huge denominational organizations in this world.

Imagine Jesus Christ coming into this world, and having entered into His Mission of earth, organized a mega-church or super grand cathedral of 300,000 to 2, 000,000 souls in one building.

He would be the head and tail of this organization, and would have thousands of workers under Him. But the Son of God was opposed to this set-up, and cared not for it in the Kingdom of His Father. Instead, He had a small group of people who are mostly men, and handful women, who served and ministered to Him out of their meager earnings. (Lk.8:2-3) Jesus Christ who is supposed to be the Head of the Church had less than 20 people in His entourage or fellowship. How do we see it in today's world? The concept of House Churches made sense, and it calls for the proliferations of House Churches all over the world.

He did not set up for Himself a super kingdom, but deferred to His Father and God. This should be the attitude of the Ministers of the Gospel of our Lord Jesus Christ, but they differed from Christ, the Head of His Church. It was pride, arrogance and the insatiable quest in the human heart, given by the spirit of Satan to walk on the wrong courses. The Church in the 21st century needs to go back to the 1st century, and begin again in House Churches, spreading His everlasting Gospel.

I believe that this is the heart of God, and He wants us to begin walking in His ways, and speak His Words like the 1st century saints, who were martyred by the world of the ungodly. Let each mega church, super cathedral, colossal church center, and all in between buy into the mind of Christ, like His first apostles and disciples of the 1st century. God is well able to support His works and ministers, and they will not lack for money, resources and wealth. The Lord, our God is still the One who gives us the power to makes wealth. (Deut.8:17-18)

WHY HOUSE CHURCHES?

Home Churches provide a simple and wonderful alternative to attending traditional Church. The Churches in the New Testament were home Churches. Throughout the centuries, many people have met in homes. There are millions of people who are having Church in homes today, but you rarely hear of them, because they are not advertised, neither are they high profile. There are many reasons to have Church in Homes. Here are a few of the primary reasons:

1. House Church is Biblical.
2. The essence of Christianity is easily accomplished in simple and uncomplicated settings.
3. Group participation with all people functioning should be the primary dynamic of any Church meeting. (1Cor.14) This is the backbone of the Home Church setting.
4. Connecting with others and developing meaningful relationships are easily accomplished in a Home Church atmosphere.
5. "Being the Church" and sharing life together in community with others, instead of just attending a meeting, is the desire and purpose of most people who are in the Home Church.

The challenge to people who want to participate in Home Church is to be able to "undo" what they have been taught Church is really all about. Prayer, worship, reading scripture, outreach, encouraging one another and sharing life together in real and meaningful ways are all part of the Home Church experience.

THE DESIRE OF GOD

In Jerusalem, when the Gospel had saturated the city, God wanted the apostles to spread out into the regions and cities of the world. They were to go to Judea, Samaria and the uttermost parts of the planet. But they have quickly forgotten the mandate of the Lord Jesus Christ given to them. The mandate stated: "But you shall receive power, after that the Holy Ghost is come upon you: and you shall be witnesses unto Me both in Jerusalem, and in all Judea, and in Samaria, and unto the uttermost parts of the earth." (Acts.1:8)

This was the will of God, and it is still His will today, but mankind has built only three Tabernacles: one for Christ, one for Moses and one for Elijah. **We want to be stationary, and do all our evangelism in one place.** We have specialized in building mega churches, super cathedrals and colossal churches to limit and restrict the people of God, thus fencing in His Spirit, doing our own thing.

He wanted His people to saturate Jerusalem, Judea, Samaria and the six to seven million cities of our world. They vexed the Lord their God, and He sent them persecution to get them going, and scattered them. Nevertheless, the apostles still remained within the city of Jerusalem. Then, He provoked Herod Agrippa to take James, the bother of John, and he was sawn asunder, putting him to death. He then proceeded to take Peter, intending to bring him out after the Passover to the people for public execution.

The Church, therefore organized prayer vigil, and sought the face of the Lord to spare Peter's life. This action sent the apostles going every- where, and they carried the Gospel with them. God never intended that the saints of God should gather together in one mega structure built by man, and expect the sinners to come in. God wanted His people to go to the world, and as they meet in houses, in staggering numbers of millions of millions, in the small groups of 2-15-20, they will begin to call the sinners into their homes within each city.

They will be faceless, but very faithful to Jesus Christ their Lord. They will not have name, except the name of the city where they meet. It will be the Church in Chicago, London, Paris, Tokyo, Madrid, Lagos, Winnipeg, Brandon, Vancouver, New York, Caracas, Kuala Lumpur, Timbuktu and all the cities of our world.

Can you imagine such an explosion of power, faith, the word of God, righteousness, peace, holiness, revelation, wisdom, divine dreams and the explosion of the Spirit of God on planet earth? The writer of this book seeks God for the days like these, when the Church will arise in power, glory, righteousness, visions and all the graces of God. He joins with all the saints to say: "Maranatha, come Lord Jesus Christ, come, and save us from ourselves, and from the saints who are carrying out the agenda of themselves and the enemy.

PLURAL SERVANTS LEADERSHIP IN HIS CHURCH

The Church was officially the Bride of Christ when His blood was shed on earth, and received in heaven in the Tabernacle not made with human hands. From that time on, the Church became part and parcel of Christ. Christ is the Head, and the Church, His Body. Christ and His Church became inseparable from then until eternity. He ordained five offices of servant leaders for His Church. These servant leaders will always be plural in number, not singular, representing and functioning under the Chief Shepherd and Apostle of His Church. (1Pet.2:25, Heb.3:1)

In today's 21st century Church where there are master leaders of His Church, it is an abnormal set to have these larger than life ministers who have laid claims to the leadership of His Church. They say that God spoke to them, and that only them as His spokesman, like Moses, can hear and direct His Church. The era of Moses in the OT was different from that of Christ in the NT. Christ instituted a new order, and this was confirmed in Heb.8-10. Of all the different Churches that the apostles and the apostolic workers had established as they were being used of God's Spirit, gave the glory to God and His Christ. They laid no claims to the Church of the Lord Jesus Christ. There was no of them who had a single, authoritative leadership, who thought that the Church was his. The Church belongs to Jesus Christ, and He is building her. (Matt.16:18)

As we can see from Jerusalem to the Seven Churches of Revelation, (Rev.2-3) they all had plural leaderships. In Jerusalem, the Church had apostles and elders who presided over His Church as servant leaders. (Acts.15:4) Matters like doctrinal issues were resolved by them as in the case of whether the Gentile saints should be circumcised or not. (Acts.15) One of the most difficult things to do is being a disciple of Christ, and living like a Jew under the OT Laws. The saints of Christ who were Jews found this so difficult, especially James, the half brother of the Lord. (Gal.2 and Acts.13:39-41) Paul had so much difficulty in this area though he talked extensively on it. (Acts.8:1, Chapters 13-28) He was always going back to the Jews, and never did fulfilled his mandate given him by the Lord in Acts.9:15-16.

Some leaders always wanted the Church to live as if they are Jews, and wanted the saints to observe important Jewish Festivals given to them by God under Moses. If the saints would do this, we might as well return to the Temple Sacrifices and the blood of bulls and goats that God called unacceptable to Him. (Heb.8-10) In Heb.12:18 and 22, the Scriptures used two phrases: "You Are Not Come and You Are Come", signifying the Old and New Covenants. We have not come under the Law of Moses of vv.18-21, but we have come into the New Covenant of Christ as of vv.22-24.

In the Church of Jesus Christ, there should be plural leaderships like Acts.13:1, a model given to us in Acts.15:4. They were prophets, teachers and apostles, a total of five leaders. The Spirit of God was in there midst, and there was harmony amongst the five of them. They did not argue as to who would preach the sermon next Sunday. God spoke to them by His Spirit, and all things were in order. It is so beautiful to behold when God is amongst His people. This is how His Church should function on earth, but power, pride, money and prestige have made those who should be servant leaders to be larger than life single leaders of the individual Church He died for. They have founded and established these Churches by their own wisdom, strength and power. They are dictatorial and authoritative, lording it over the Household of Faith, which is the Pillar of Truth. (1Tim.3:15)

Jesus Christ came to show the world a new way of service in God regarding His Church. He set up the servant leader model for us all to follow after His steps. He said, "The Son of Man is come, not to be ministered unto or served, but to serve, and give His Life a ransom for many". (Mk.10:42-45, Matt.20:25-26) If you are a teacher, pastor, evangelist, prophet or an apostle, and you took the office of a bishop that Christ did not give, you have demoted yourself, and have fallen from grace to grass, and from frying pan to fire. You are after the honor of men, and not the honor that comes from God.

The heart of the NT leadership is service and servant-hood as opposed to being authoritative and dictatorial in ministering to the people of God. When we look at James and John, the sons of Zebedee, Peter, Andrew, Paul and the rest of the apostles, and the disciples of Christ, we see this model of a servant leader in their leaderships, and not one who barks at the people of God, and beat them with the rod of God's Word in order to take money from them. It is anathema to the Spirit of Christ, and His Church.

Ministering is a privilege that the Lord of the Church has given to us, His servants and ministers, and we must not abuse this opportunity. Paul admonished Timothy, Titus, Gaius, the apostolic entourage, and others to carefully appoint or ordain workers, elders and bishops in every Church they had established through the Spirit of God. They were used by God's Spirit as servant leaders, and not as slave masters of His Church.

The Gentile Church sent a relief to the saints at Jerusalem through the elders of the Church. (Acts.11:30) Paul and Barnabas appointed "ELDERS" in every Church. (Acts.14:21-23) Paul called for the leadership of the Church at Ephesus. (Acts.20:17) Timothy, Titus and Gaius were instructed to appoint elders in every Church. Leadership is always plural in number, and not the assistant pastors that we have today, who are subordinate to the larger than life senior pastors. Paul admonished the saints to respect, honor and minister to those who served/rule over them. He referred to these men as "THEM" indicating a plurality of servant leaders. (Heb.13:7, 14 and 24)

Finally, it is not biblical nor is it Scriptural to have authority and dominion over the people of God in an authoritative manner, lording it over them. Jesus Christ said, "The princes of the Gentiles exercise authority/dominion over them, but it shall not be so among you". (Matt.20:25-26) Christ manifested a servant leader model for His Church, and He said, "The Son of man is not come to be ministered unto, but to minister, and give His Life a ransom for many". (vv.27-28)

James, one of the elders in Jerusalem Church was writing to encourage the Church in diaspora, and he said, "Is any sick among you? Let him call for the "**elders**" of the Church; and let "**them**" pray over him, anointing him with oil in the name of the Lord." (Jms.5:14-15) Here one can see that the leadership of the Church is plural, and the terms "ELDERS and THEM" were used instead of senior pastor and him. The NT Church has never been an individual exerting his authority over the people of God as Moses did, because he was in a different dispensation. We are in the last days, and it is one love, grace and pluralistic leadership. The word says, "Without counsel purposes are disappointed, but in the multitude of counselors they are established". (Pro.15:22)

Chapter Five

THE BIBLICAL DEFINITION AND PURPOSE OF THE CHURCH

DR. DUK SOO JANG
(Liberty Baptist Theological Seminary)
By Permission

Many people today understand the Church as a building. This is not a biblical understanding of the Church. The basic definition of the Church is the people who are called by God in Christ. (Col.1:1, 2; Eph.2:19) This becomes clearer if the meaning of the word "Church" is examined more closely. The Church, which is God's people called out of the world, can be described as the living, systematic, and public expression of God's sovereignty initiated by Christ's incarnation.

The New Testament contains more than 100 instances of words, parables, and symbols indicating the Church. The word "Church" is derived from the Greek word kuriakos, belonging to the Lord. But, this is to be understood in the light of the New Testament Greek term eklesia, which is defined as "an assembly" or "called-out ones." It is derived from the verb ekkaleo, a compound of ek, "out," and kaleo, "to call or summon."

More specifically, this word contains the meaning of the process of the congregation coming together and the community of people already gathered in one place. Therefore, the Church is a chosen generation and a holy nation. (1Pet.2:9) God gave birth to His people. (Jn.1:12-13) He made, called, preserved, and saved them. This Church of God, concept began, after the resurrection of Christ with those who confessed that He is Christ and God's own Son. They are new creatures that have been removed from the power of darkness and brought into the kingdom of the Son of God. (Col.1:13)

The Church in a period of transition, however, should earnestly and humbly wait for the kingdom of God, so that she will be perfected in the future, when the Lord returns. The Church has not yet arrived at her final destination, but is on her pilgrimage toward the eternal city. The present Church, therefore, is a signpost that announces the end, and a billboard that reveals what is to come. When the King comes, the Church will inherit the kingdom and this kingdom will be realized throughout the whole universe.

THE THEOLOGICAL DEFINITION OF A CHURCH

The Church is a New Testament doctrine and the word "Church" never appears in the Old Testament. In the Old Testament, the people are only the Jews, while in the New Testament, the people of God are gathered from every ethnic background into a new community which are Jews and Gentiles. Charles Ryrie asserts that she is built upon Jesus' resurrection, for the Lord was made head of the Church, after God "raised Christ from the dead, and set him at his own right hand in the heavenly places." (Eph.1:20) The writer of the first Gospel used the Greek word ekklesia to describe Christ's "Church." (Matt.16:18)

The Church was introduced and initiated by Jesus Christ. In Matt.16:18, Christ said, "I will build My Church." In using the future tense, Jesus was not saying, as some contend, that He had build His Church in the past.

Matt.18:20, Jesus points out at least seven features and characteristics of the Church that He will build. He speaks of her foundation, her certainty, her intimacy, her identity and her continuity, her invincibility, her authority, and her spirituality." First, Jesus set forth the foundation of the Church: And I also say to you that you are Peter, and upon this Rock, I will build My Church. For more than fifteen hundred years, the Roman Catholic Church has maintained that this passage teaches the Church was built on the person of Peter, who became the first pope and bishop of Rome, and from whom the Catholic papacy has since descended. Because of this supposed divinely ordained apostolic succession, the pope is considered to be the supreme and authoritative representative of Christ on earth. Such an interpretation, however, is presumptuous and unbiblical, because the rest of the New Testament makes abundantly clear that Christ alone is the foundation, and only the head of His Church. (1Cor.3:11)

Second, Jesus pointed out the certainty of the Church, declaring, "I will build My Church." It will, fanatical, ritualistic, apathetic, or apostate its outward adherents may be, and no matter how decadent the rest of the world may become, Christ will build His Church, and the leadership of hell will not over power her.

Scriptures quoted will be from the New International Version, unless otherwise noted. Church, therefore, no matter how oppressive and hopeless their outward circumstances may appear from a human perspective, God's people belong to a cause that cannot be built by man. It is the divine promise of the divine Savior.

Third, Jesus alluded to the intimacy of the fellowship. "It is My Church," His followers that they are His personal possession and eternally have His divine love and care. They are His body, "purchased with His own blood." (Acts.20:28)

Forth, Jesus emphasized the identity and continuity of His people. They are His Church. The word ekklesia literally means "the called out ones" and was used as a general and nontechnical term for any officially assembled group of people. (Who made that decision?)

Fifth, Jesus spoke of the invincibility of the Church, which the gate of Hades shall not overpower. Its gates are not strong enough to overpower and keep imprisoned the Church of God, whose Lord has conquered sin and death on her behalf. (Rom.8:2; Acts.2:24) Because "death no longer is master over Him." (Rom.6:9) It is no longer master over those who belong to Him. "Because I live," Jesus said, "you shall live also." (Jn.14:19)

Sixth, Jesus spoke about the authority of the Church. "I will give you the keys of the kingdom of heaven," He said; "and whatever you shall bind on earth, shall be bound in heaven, and whatever you shall loose on earth, shall be loosed in heaven."

Finally, Jesus reminds the disciples that His Church is a spiritual reality, as He warned them that they should tell no one that He was the Christ. Elmer Towns defines the word Church in the theological definition in the following terms:

1. Church is an assembly of professing believers
2. The unique presence of Jesus Christ dwells in the Church
3. A Church is under the discipline of the Word of God
4. A Church is organized to carry out the Great Commission
5. A Church administers the ordinances
6. A Church reflects the spiritual gifts.

The first characteristic of a New Testament Church is that it is an assembly of those who have their faith in Jesus Christ. (Rom.10:9) Regeneration is the prime requisite for membership in the Church. On the day of Pentecost, those who believed were immediately baptized and added to the Church. (Acts.2:41)

Second, Jesus Christ dwells in the midst of His people. "For where two or three are gathered together in My name, I am there in the midst of them." (Matt.18:20) Yet, Christ does more than indwell His Church; He is the organic Head of His Church. She is His body and He is her Head.

Third, doctrinal commitment is essential for a New Testament Church. One of the first religious exercises of the New Testament Church after the day of Pentecost was that "they continued steadfastly in the apostles' doctrine". (Acts.2:42) There is a unique union between Christ and the Word, for both are the Breath of God.

Fourth, the early Church "did not cease teaching and preaching Jesus as the Christ". (Acts.5:42) Because the Church is an organized body existing to fulfill the Great Commission and everyone outside of Christ is lost, a Church must have an effectively organized program for evangelism and discipleship to edify or build up those who are a part of her.

Fifth, a Church exercises the two ordinances, baptism, (Rom. 6:4-6) and the Lord's Super. (1Cor.11:23-26) These are to be celebrated by the Church when it assembles together. Baptism signifies both the response of faith on the part of the one baptized, and the salvation act of God, performed in response to faith. The Lord's Supper is important because it does the remembrance of Jesus Christ, (Lk.22:19; 1Cor.11:24-25) and is a present fellowship with Christ.

Sixth, every Christian receives the spiritual gifts from the Holy Spirit. (1Cor.12:11) The Spirit is the agent who gives gift, and the believers may have a part in the development of his or her gifts.

It is also the Spirit who works all these things. Therefore, the Spirit is the messenger of the Head of the Church, giving and energizing the spiritual gifts as deity has designed.

THE DESCRIPTION OF THE CHURCH IN THE SCRIPTURE

The New Testament presents the Church both in literal terms and in rich metaphorical descriptions. This richness of descriptions precludes a narrow concept of the Church, and warns against magnification of one aspect to disregard of others.

THE CHURCH AS THE BODY OF CHRIST (1COR.12:12-27)

Perhaps the most extended image of the Church is its representation as the body of Christ. Paul develops the extended metaphor of the Church as the body of Christ that makes the Church equal to Christ as an extension of His incarnation.

Through verse 27 of chapter 12, Paul uses the term body some 16 times, and he uses the metaphor in many other places in his writings. (Rom.12:5; Eph.1:23; 2:16; 4:4, 12, 16; Col.1:18; etc.) **The human body is by far the most amazing organic creation of God. It is marvelously complex, yet unified, with unparalleled harmony and inter-relatedness. It is a unit; it cannot be subdivided into several bodies. If it is divided, the part that is cut off ceases to function and dies, and the rest of the body loses some of its functions and effectiveness.** The body is immeasurably more than the sum of its parts.

The Church as an organism is the complex structure of the body of Christ that carries on living activities by means of the individual believers who are distinct in function, but knit together and governed by their relation to Christ, the Head. Christ's Body is also one. There are many Christian organizations, denominations, agencies, clubs, and groups of every sort. But there is only one Church, of which every true believer in Christ is a member. While He was on earth, Christ was incarnated in a single body. Now, He is incarnated in another body, the great, diverse, and precious Body that is His Church.

There is no true Church life without Christ life. Paul did not say, "For to me, to live is being a Christian," but "For me, to live is Christ". (Phil.1:21) He could say, in fact, "It is no longer I who live, but Christ lives in me". (Gal.2:20) **This same Christ's life is possessed by every believer, and every believer therefore, is a part of Christ, a part of His Body, the Church. Therefore, the part cannot separate themselves from the body, so that as long as there is a body of Christ, it must be one.** (Eph.4:11-13)

THE CHURCH AS THE PEOPLE OF GOD

Even when we know better, we tend to think of the Church as either a physical structure or a denominational entity, both of which exist to programs. The Church, however, is an assembly of people that are the elect of God. According to Saucy, the Church as God's assembly, is founded upon the "counsel" and "good pleasure of His will", (Eph.1:5, 11) and "chosen (elected) in Him (Christ) before the foundation of the world". (Eph.1:4) As such, the members of the Church are "God's elect", (Rom.8:33; Col.3:12) or simply "the elect" (1Pet.1:2; 2Tim.2:10) "an elect race", (1Pet.2:9) "the called" of God, (Rom.1:6; 8:28; 1Cor. 1:24; Rev.17:14) and "a people for God's own.

Saucy also states that the Church is the member of Christ, and that the eternal purpose of God becomes clear in the historical person of Christ. The roots of the new community were planted in His command: "follow me." From a band of disciples, His followers became the nucleus of the Church that acknowledged Him as Lord and Savior, for the Church owed her very existence to His person and work. If we remember that the Church is the people, several implications follow.

First, Church is no longer perceived as a program that some people put on for others to watch. The people are participants, joining together to worship and have fellowship with God, who is present with them as a group.

Second, Ministry is for everyone, not merely the clergy. The people are the temple in which God dwells.

Third, value is placed on people. Sometimes the impression is given that people are dispensable, as long as the building is maintained, and the programs keep going. The average Church in Korea devotes the majority of her funds to her building and internal operations. What if they invested in people as much as in our buildings and systems?

THE CHURCH AS THE TEMPLE OF THE HOLY SPIRIT

This metaphor describes two things. First, in 1Cor.6:19, Paul says, "Your body is the temple of the Holy Spirit, who is in you." As Christians, our bodies are not our own. Paul puts sting into this verse by framing it as a sarcastic question.

They are the Lord's, members of Christ, and temples of the Holy Spirit, who has been given by God to indwell us. So he calls for sexual purity, not only because of the way sexual sin affects the body, but because the body it affects is not even the believer's own. Understanding the reality of the phrase, the Holy Spirit who is in you, whom you have from God, should give us as much commitment to purity, as any knowledge of divine truth could. Every act of fornication, every act of adultery by Christians, is committed in God's sanctuary: their own bodies "for we are the temple of the living God." (2Cor.6:16) The fact that Christians are the dwelling place of the Holy Spirit is indicated in passages such as Jn.7:38-39; 20:22; Acts.1:8; Rom.8:9; and 1Cor.12:3.

The fact that God sent the Holy Spirit is clear from Jn.14:16-17; 15:26; and Acts.2:17, 33, 38.

We no longer belong to ourselves, because we have been bought with a price. We were not "redeemed with perishable things like silver or gold from our futile way of life, inherited from our forefathers, but with the precious blood, as of a lamb unblemished and spotless, the blood of Christ". (1Pet.1:18-19) Christians' Bodies are God's Temple, and a Temple is for worship. Our bodies, therefore, have one supreme purpose: to glorify God. This is a call to live so as to bring honor to the Being of God, who alone is worthy of our obedience and adoration.

Second, in 1Cor.3:11, Paul used the metaphor of a building as he wrote of the Church. The foundation Paul laid as a wise Builder, was that of Christ Himself, and His teaching. Some builders have tried to make the foundation of Christianity to be Church's tradition, others, the moral teachings of the human Jesus, others ethical humanism, and still others, some form of pseudo-scientism or simply sentimental love and good works. But the only foundation of the Church and of Christian living is Jesus Christ. Without this foundation no spiritual building will be God's or will stand.

The figure of the building or temple of God bears similarities to that of the body, such as the spiritual gifts are given to edify or build up the body, and the building grows. (Eph.2:21) Not only is the building built on Christ Jesus, the Cornerstone, the whole building exists in Him as well.

In Him the building is bound together and grows into a temple in Him; in Him the Gentiles are built together with the Jews to be a dwelling of God in the Spirit. The joining together of the elements that make up the total structure of this new divine community is an ongoing activity. The new community of God is growing and progressing to her ultimate goal, because the character of the New Building is derived from God who inhabits her.

THE CHURCH AS THE BRIDE OF CHRIST

One of the most beautiful images of the Church is that of the bride of Christ. For example, Rev.21:19 says, "Come here, I shall show you the bride, the wife of the Lamb. For I am jealous for you with a godly jealousy; for I betrothed you to one husband, that is to Christ, that I might present you as a pure virgin." (2Cor.11:2) Also, in Eph.5:22-23, Paul uses the union of Christ and His Church to illustrate the relation of husband and wife.

As human marriage involves the intimacy of oneness, the members of the Church are united to Christ as "members of His body, of His flesh, and of His bones". (Eph.5:30) Dr. Towns says that the major part of the teaching of the picture of the bride and groom is her demonstration of Christ's limitless love.

The Evidence of love from a husband to his wife is his concern for her welfare. A loving husband nourishes and cherishes his wife as he does his own body. This idea means Christ as the bridegroom, nourishes and cherishes His bride, supplying her with every necessity for health and welfare. (Eph.5:29)

Then, what should be the response of the bride? The Church as the bride must be subject unto Christ, even as the wife is to the husband in the marriage relationship. The wife's supreme motive for submitting to her husband is the fact that he is her functional head in the family, just as Christ also is the head of the Church. (1Cor.11:3; Col.1:18; Eph.1:22-23)

The head gives direction and the body responds. A physical body that does not respond to the direction of the head is crippled, paralyzed, or spastic. Likewise, a wife who does not properly respond to the direction of her husband, manifests a serious spiritual dysfunction.

THE CHURCH AS THE FLOCK OF GOD

The metaphor of the shepherd and His flock is used in the Old Testament and New Testament. In the Old Testament, Israel is called "the Lord's flock." (Jer.13:17; cf. Zech.10:13) God is the Shepherd, who loves and tenderly cares for His sheep. "The Lord is my shepherd". (Psm.23:1) "Please listen, O Shepherd of Israel, you who lead Joseph's descendants like a flock." (Psm.80:1; cf. Isa.40:11; Exo.19:3-8; Psm.100:3)

The flock of the New Testament Church is composed of sheep from both Israel and the Gentiles. Jesus referred to His small circle of disciples as the "little flock". (Lk.12:32) Again the term is used of the Church on several occasions. (cf. Acts.20:38; 1Pet.5:3) In addition to these, there are the repeated references to the sheep that compose of the flock. (Jn.10:2-16; 1Pet.2:25; 5:4; and Heb.13:20) The prominent concept involved in the metaphor of the flock of God is the ownership of the flock.

Jesus declared, "My sheep hear My voice". (Jn.10:27) Jesus purchased His ownership with His own blood. (Acts.20:28) Christ, the Shepherd has not only purchased the Church, but He also provides for her every need. He guards the sheep from danger, tends the sick, searches for the lost, and above all, leads them to good and green pasture.

A primary task of the Shepherd is, however, the provision of nourishment—metaphorically, His spiritual nourishment of His sheep that is accomplished through the ministry of the Word. (2Tim.4:2; 3:16-17; Acts.20:27)

THE PURPOSE OF THE CHURCH

The following are some different views of the purpose of the Church. Craig Van Gelder says that the purposes of the

Church of the Lord are: (1) "People of God": the Church is to live in reconciled relationship with God, and one another, as a new creation. (2) "The body of Christ": the Church is to live as a unified community in sacrificial love and fellowship. "Communion of saints": we now experience God and each other in reconciled relationships based on what we share in common in Christ. "Creation of the Spirit": the Church is always in process, and will exhibit characteristics of organizational and institutional life.

George Peters suggests three missions of the Church: (1) The upward purpose is based on the fact of who God is, and the Church of Jesus Christ. This includes worship, adoration, praise, and intercession. (2) The inward purpose includes fellowship, education, edification, and discipline. (3) The outward purpose to the world includes; evangelism, service, instruction, and reproof. Though he states many lists in his "three missions" of the Church, they can be summarized into: worship, discipleship, and evangelism.

Millard Erickson presents four purposes with which the Church is charged to carry out: (1) Evangelism: if the Church is to be faithful to her Lord and bring joy to His heart, she must be engaged in bringing the gospel to all people, (2) Edification: although Jesus laid greater emphasis upon evangelism, Erickson says, the edification of believers is logically prior, (3) Worship: it concentrates upon the Lord, and (4) Social concern: Christians have responsibility to perform acts of Christian love, kindness and compassion for both believers and non-Christians.

Personally, Warren states the best explanation of the purposes of the Church. He mentions five tasks for the Church after observing two statements by Jesus: the Great Commandments, (Matt.23:37-40) and the Great Commission. (Matt.28:19-20) (1) Love the Lord with all your heart: worship (intimacy) (2) Love your neighbor as yourself: ministry (service) (3) Go and make disciples: evangelism (mission) (4) Baptize them: (fellowship) (5) Teach them to obey: (discipleship).

SUMMARY

A Church is the only hope of the world and is the community of salvation. It is not a building, but a gathering of God's people. God wants to accomplish His will through the Church. Jesus taught us to pray, "Your will be done on earth as it is in heaven" (Matt.6:9). God wants His will to be done on earth through the Church. That is why He is building His Church on earth. Thus, the Church should realize the five purposes of her existence on earth, so that God's will may be done on earth. She also needs to do her best to fulfill her God-given calling. First, the Church exists to worship God. The Bible says, "Worship the Lord your God, and serve him only." (Matt.4:10)

Worshiping God is Church's number one purpose. Through Scripture, we are commanded to celebrate God's presence by magnifying the Lord and exalting his name. "O magnify the Lord with me and let us exalt his name together." (Psm.34:3) We should not worship out of duty; we should worship, because we want to. We should enjoy expressing our love to God.

Second, the Church exists to minister to people. Ministry is demonstrating God's love to others by meeting their needs, and healing their hurts in the name of Jesus. The Church is to minister to all kinds of needs: spiritual, emotional, relational, and physical. Jesus said that even a cup of cold water given in his name was considered as ministry and would not go unrewarded. The Church is to "equip the saints for the work of ministry." (Eph.4:12 NRSV)

Third, the Church exists to communicate God's Word. We are ambassadors for Christ, and our mission is to evangelize the world. Evangelism is more than our responsibility; it is our great privilege and supreme task.

Fourth, the Church exists to provide fellowship for believers. As Christians, we are called to belong, not just to believe. We are not meant to live lone-ranger lives; instead, we are to belong to Christ's family and be members of his body. We are not alone. We have each other for support. Notice that worship comes before services.

Lastly, the Church exists to educate God's people. Discipleship is the process of helping people become more like Christ in their thoughts, feelings, and actions. This process begins when a person is born again, and continues throughout the rest of his life. Col.1:28 (NCV) says, "We continue to preach Christ to each person, using all wisdom to warn and to teach everyone, in order to bring each one into God's presence, as a mature person in Christ"

Chapter Six

GOD'S TABERNACLE

(BEFORE SPIRITS AND ANGELS)

In the eons of time past, before angels were created, God dwelt in a Temple not made with hands, as hands were not even around yet. What kind of Temple was God living in, knowing that He neither slumbers nor sleeps? No human mind can ever capture the essence, because man was in no place to be found yet.

God lives with spirit beings, and they were not angels, who were created out of the mind of God. He had a Temple for the spirits to gather for His worship, yet the spirits were the Temple. God does not need a physical structure for the spirit beings to worship Him. He fills the heaven of heavens, and all of the physical worlds. He needed nothing.

Worship was flowing like an ever-pure river of gold, between the spirits, and flowing from Him to them like an ever-increasing sweet smelling perfume of the highest order, made by God Himself. The mind of man cannot even describe it, let alone, feel its flow and power. He was not around to imagine it.

Let us fast-forward the government of God, and put angels and men into this equation several billion of years to come. Both angels and men will be at a loss at the marvelous and magnificent wisdom of our God. Even now in the 21st century, it has not entered into the hearts of men, ears of men have not heard, and the spirits of men have not received it, as to the beautiful things God is preparing for those that loved Him, in the purity of their hearts. (1Cor.1:9ff)

We don't know much about this God who has revealed Himself to our spirits in His Son Jesus Christ. It takes spirit to know spirit, and except God by His own Spirit will reveal His heart to mankind, we will be in darkness as to the revelation, knowledge, wisdom, understanding, compassion and the love of our God.

How did the spirits then, worship God? I am not talking about the angel, but spirit beings, before the angels that we know today. What were the instruments they used in worshipping this God? They have their whole beings as instruments of worship, and there is no one like them in angelic and human history put together. It beats angelic mind, not to talk about our puny, little and fragile minds in the things that God had and has before angels and mankind.

When He created both angels and mankind, and gave them the responsibility to worship Him, we are still not up to the task where we can satisfactorily worship Him, who needed nothing from His creations, except to do this, in spirit and in truth.

So, what was His Tabernacle like? What about His throne? Is there a resemblance to it in all of the lower heavens and on the earth below? Human imagination pales at the mentioning of the Tabernacle in heaven, at that time, before angels. All that the author can say to the magnificence of this God is: "I am glad that He came to bring us to His standard, and apart from this benevolence, we can never measure up to the standards of our God. I am so glad that Christ came to our infinitesimally small earth, to seek and save us for His Father, God.

When He decided to create angels, and later mankind, at the fall of the third of the angelic hosts of heaven, He stooped down to us earthlings, and sent His Son to appear before us, who deserved to die and perish. The author marveled at the wisdom of our God in planning our redemption and salvation for His glory and praise. No wonder the Scripture says, **"His mercy endures forever." (Psm.107:1ff)**

There was no silence, and it was a constant crescendo of praises in a place that knew no night and day, and yet, every thing was in perfect harmony, as they gently sang His worth in cascading symphonies of worship, praise and honor of the majesty of our God, forever and ever. Incredible and unbelievable to behold! **The author was not even there.**

That God will ask and give mortal men a place in this euphoria of heaven was totally unimaginable to mankind. That man will one day join the spirits beings, angels and the arch-angels in procession of worship to this great God, who has no equal in all of the seven heavens, the worlds and our earth is beyond our comprehension as men.

When this happens, pride, selfishness, wealth, arrogance, and all we hold dear will pale at the revelation of our God, King and Father, who gave us His Son, to be the propitiation for our sins. Christ always did the will of His Father, and when He said a thing, that was the will of Him that sent Him. Why did Jesus Christ not build a mega structure or a super cathedral on planet earth? It was not the will of His Father to do so, otherwise, He would have been following the examples of the head of the angels, Lucifer, himself.

Christ did what would please His Father, and did so even unto His death. No wonder the Father said of the Son, "This is My beloved Son in whom I AM well pleased. There was no sin in Him, and this is why He became the Champion and Captain of mankind's salvation, from the wrath of God and the powers of darkness. No wonder the Father has given Him a name that is above all names, that at the name of Jesus Christ, all knees should bow: of heaven, on earth, below the earth, and wherever the knees of man, spirits, angels and beast are, they are commanded to bow down at the mentioning of the name of Jesus Christ, the Son of God.

Chapter Seven

YOU ARE INVINCIBLE

(THE CHURCH: HIS EXTENSION ON EARTH)

The Lord Jesus Christ is the builder and owner of His Church. He has declared that His Church on the earth is of a divine origin, and as such, she is victorious, undefeatable, and more than conquerors. (Rom.8:37)

> These are what He said that
> His Church should say about
> Herself.

We are who God says we are. We are the salt of the earth. (Matt.5:13) We are the light of the world. (Matt.5:14) We are the children of God. (Jn.1:12) We are parts of the True Vine, and channels of Christ's Life. (Jn.15:1, 5)

We are Christ's friends. (Jn.15:15) We are chosen in Him, and appointed by Him to bear His fruit. (Jn.15:16) We are slaves of righteousness, and enslaved to our God. (Rom.6:18, 22) We are sons and daughters of the Living God, and joint heirs with Christ. (Gal.3:26; Rom.8:14-15, 17) We are the Temple of God, and members of Christ's body. (1Cor.12:27; Eph.5:30)

We are united with the Lord, and we are one with Jesus Christ. (1Cor.6:17) We are new creation in Him, and have been reconciled to God, our Father. (2Cor.5:17) We are ministers of reconciliation from Christ to mankind. (2Cor.5:18-20) We have been crucified with Christ, and we live by His faith. (Gal.2:20)

We are one with Christ, and heirs of God. (Gal.3:26, 28; 4:6-7) We are the saints of God, and Christ's ambassadors. (Eph.1:1; 1Cor.1:2) We are God's workmanship, and we have become to Him His handiwork. (Eph.2:10) We are born anew in Christ to do His work, and we are citizens with the saints, God's family on earth. (Eph.2:19) We are prisoners of Christ, and we are righteous and holy. (Eph.3:1, 4:1 and 4:24)

We are citizens of heaven, and are seated in heaven at the presence of God right now. (Phil.2:6, 3:20) Our lives are hidden with Christ in God, and we are an expression of the Life of Christ. He is our life. (Col.3:3-4) We are chosen of God, holy and dearly beloved in Christ. (Col.3:12; 1Thes.1:4) We are the children of light, and not of darkness. (1Thes.5:5)

We are holy partakers of a heavenly calling in Christ, and we share in His Life. (Heb.3:1, 14) We are one of God's living stones, and we are being built up in Christ as a spiritual house of the Lord. (1Pet.2:5) We are members of a chosen race, a royal priesthood, a holy nation, and a people for God's own possession. (1Pet.2:9-10)

We are aliens and strangers to this world in which we temporarily live, and we are the enemies of the devil, called Satan. (1Pet.2:11, 5:8) We are the children of God, and we resemble Christ right now, and hereafter. (1Jn.3:1-2) We are born of God, and Satan cannot touch us, because we are justified, forgiven and made righteous in Him. (Rom.5:1; 1Jn.5:18)

We are dead in Christ, and are dead to the power of sin's rule over our lives. (Rom.6:1-6) We are free forever from all condemnations, because the Spirit of life in Christ Jesus has made us free from the law of sin and death. (Rom.8:1) We are placed into Christ body by God's doing, and we are in possession of the Spirit of God in our lives that we might know the things that are freely given to us by God. (1Cor.2:12) We are in possession of the mind of Christ, therefore, we can do all things by His power working in us. (1Cor.2:16; Phil.4:13)

We are bought with a price, we are not our own, we belong to Christ in God. (1Cor.6:19-20) We are established, anointed and sealed by God in Christ. God has given us His Spirit as a pledge, guaranteeing our inheritance to come. (1Cor.1:21; Eph.1:13-14)

We are living right here and now for Christ, and we are made righteous in Him. (2Cor.5:14-15, 21) We are blessed with every spiritual blessing in the heavenly places in Him, and we are chosen in Him before the foundation of the world. (Eph.1:3-4)

We are holy and blameless before God, our Father, and we have been redeemed and forgiven. We are the recipients of God lavish grace. (Eph.1:4, 6-8) We are alive in Christ, and are risen and seated with Him in heaven, therefore, we have been given access to God's throne, through His Spirit and by the Blood of Christ. (Eph.2:5, 6, 18)

We are confident in His confidence, and we do approach God with boldness and freedom. (Eph.3:12) We are transferred into the Kingdom of Christ, and have been rescued from the domain of Satan's rule. (Col.1:13) We are redeemed and forgiven of all our sins, therefore, we are in Christ, and Christ is in us. (Col.1:14, 27) We are firmly rooted in Christ, and we are being built up in Him, therefore, we are complete in Christ, our Lord. (Col.2:7, 10)

We are buried with Christ, and raised up in Him. Our lives are now hidden with Christ in God. We have double insulation in

God. He is our Life. (Col.3:1-4) We are in possession of the Spirit's power, love and self-discipline. (2Tim.1:7) We are saved and set apart according to God's doing. (2Tim.1:9; Titus.3:5) We are sanctified, and one with the Sanctifier. Christ is not ashamed to call us His brothers and sisters. (Heb.2:11)

We are God's children, therefore, we have the right to come boldly before the throne of God to receive mercy, and find grace to help us in time of need. (Heb.4:16) We are partakers of His divine nature, therefore, we have been given precious and magnificent promises by God. (2Pet.1:4)

The Church is seated with Christ in the high places where God dwells, and she has to believe this statement, or else it will not be so to her. The body of Christ on earth must trust in the Lord, and explicitly believe in what He has uttered concerning her. As He is in this world, so are we, regardless of the sight and sound on earth today.

The mystery of Christ and the Church is unfathomable by mankind. There is something secret and mysterious about Christ and His Church, and there is no one on the earth that really understands it.

The Church is married to Christ after His life and blood have been shed for her. This is marriage as God would have it, and the best on the earth cannot come close to it. This mystery union of Christ and His Church is beyond mankind. They are one flesh, and one in the Spirit. This Paul declared to be a great mystery. The mystery of godliness declared in 1Tim.3:16, stated the unreachable and unimaginable height, that the Father has gone to in bringing redemption to mankind. In Christ Jesus, God demonstrated the greatest power that both angel and mortal have ever known, heard or seen, when God raised Christ from the dead. (Eph.1:19-20)

It has never entered the ears, nor had mankind seen the exceeding great power of our God towards the Church, who has believe in Christ, according to the working of His mighty power in the Church. This power was wrought in Christ, when He raised Him from the dead, and set Him at His own right hand in the heavenly places, was the topmost power demonstrated in the anal of human history, and beyond. There will never be one like it again in this world, and the worlds to come. This power is far above all principality, power, might, dominion, majesty, and every name that is named, not only in this world, but also in that which is to come. He has put all things under His feet, and gave Him to be the head over all things to the Church. This power is beyond this world!

Chapter Eight

THE CHURCH: AN OVERCOMER

(ROM.8:31, REV.2-3)

Christ came to our world to re-create mankind who will be champions through His death, resurrection and ascension, by making them a replica of Himself. They will be transformed through His life, passion, death, burial and the resurrection from the dead. After His resurrection, He stayed with His disciples for forty days, before He returned to where He came from. He said to them, "Receive you the Holy Ghost…" (Jn.20:22) The power and force of His disciples will be like the power and force of Christ, who was sent by His Father. The Church will live just as He lived on earth. (Jn.20:11-20) They will receive the Spirit of God, just as Christ received the Spirit of His Father. (Acts.1:8, Lk.24:29) He said, "As the Father sent me, even so send I you." (Jn.20:21)

Our eyes are to be opened in order that we might know God, and our understanding needs to be enlightened that we might know and understand the words of the Lord, because He has ordained a mighty works for us on earth. (Lk.24:16, 45) There is no way the world and Satan can conquer the Church, because the scriptures maintain that she is more than conqueror, and the power of God throbs within her spirit. The Church is here to do things supernaturally, because of the Spirit of God who is in her. (Mk.16:15-18, Lk.4:18-19) The Church is to preach the Gospel to the poor, bind up the broken hearted, preach deliverance to the captive, the recovery of sight to the blind, set at liberty them that are bruised and pronounce the acceptable year of the Lord." (Isa.61:1ff) The Church will do these by the Spirit of God.

The world and Satan have no power over the Church, because Christ said, "Upon this Rock, that I am the Son of God, will I build My Church, and the gates of hell shall not prevail or over power her." (Matt.16:18-19) The Lord of the Church said to His Church in Mk.16:15-18, "Go into all the world, and preach the Gospel to every creature: he who believes and is baptized shall be saved; but he that believes not shall be damned. And these signs shall follow them that believe. In My name, they shall cast out demons, they shall speak with new tongues, they shall take up serpents and if they drink any deadly thing, it shall not hurt them. They shall lay hands on the sick, and they shall recover."

The foregoing is the investment of the Lord on the Church. She cannot be wishy-washy against sin, evil and the power of darkness. She has to stand firm under Christ to exercise all that has been written and spoken by the Lord for her. We are living in a period in which the power of hell and darkness are being released, because Satan's time is very short.

The Gospel has gone around the globe at least two times, and yet there are people who have not heard the message of life in the Gospel of our Lord Jesus Christ. One significant thing that the saints have ignored is the endowment of the Spirit of God upon the lives of the saints. If we insist on our own strength, and we continue to labor, God will let us. But if we concede and defer to the Spirit of God, the proclamation of the Gospel of Christ shall be greatly accelerated, and much will be done to hasten the coming of the Lord.

In Jn.16:33, Christ said, "These things have I spoken unto you, (that is Church) that in Me the Church might have peace. In the world, she will have tribulation, but let not your heart be troubled. Be of good cheer. I have overcome the world." In Christ, we have overcome the systems of this world and all its demonically inspired leaders. All we have to do is to open our mouths. We have overcome in Him and through Him: the world, evil, sin and the resurgence of the powers of darkness. (Rom.12:21, 1Jn.5:4 and Rev.2:7)

We have the same Spirit in us as Christ, the apostles and the first saints in Christ of the first century believers. John in his first epistle to the Church said, "I wrote to you fathers, because you have known Him that is from the beginning. I wrote unto you, young men, (and women) because you have overcome the wicked one. I wrote unto you, little children, because you have known the Father." (1Jn.2:13)

It is the knowledge and ways of God that are necessary to assure us the victory that Christ had already won for the Church to overcome the evil one. As long as the saints stayed close to the Son of God, they are with the Father, and their victory is secured. (Rev.2:11, 17:14, 3:5, 12 and 21, 21:7)

In the heroes and heroines of faith from Heb.11, we have the saints of old who have triumphed over the kingdom of darkness. Their names are enumerated for us to take courage in the race that has been set before us. Abel's blood cried out to God for vengeance, Enoch was translated that he did not see death, Noah built an Ark to save himself and his family, an evidence of the judgment of God to the then world. Abraham bored Isaac through Sarah, and both of them were over 90 years old. He believed in God against hope that the promise God gave him would come to pass. He received his son from the dead, a type of Jesus Christ, the Son of God. Also symbolized death and resurrection.

What shall we say about Isaac, Jacob, Joseph, Moses, Joshua, Rehab, Gideon, Barak, Samson, Jephthah, David, Samuel and the prophets? The Old Testament saints who through faith subdued kingdoms, wrought righteousness, obtained promises, stopped the mouths of lions, quenched the violence of fire, escaped the edge of the sword, out of weakness were made strong, waxed valiant in fight, turned to flight the armies of the aliens and on and on. (Heb.11:1-40)

The Church is a powerhouse on the earth to subdue heads of states, supernaturally, bringing peace to these warring nations of our world, and usher in the Kingdom of our God.

Chapter Nine

CHRIST TALKS TO HIS CHURCH

(REV. 2-3)
HE GAVE AN INSIDE REVELATION OF HIS CHURCH

Jesus Christ spoke to His Church when He said, "Behold my mother and my brothers. "For whosoever shall do the will of my Father who is in heaven, the same is my brother, sister and mother." (Matt.12:49-50) He was not talking to stones, bricks, nails and physical building materials.

The Church, from the declaration of the Lord here in this scripture is not a building, but human beings, made in the image and likeness of God. He said that those who would believe in Him would not perish, but have everlasting life. For God did not send His Son to condemn humanity, but that humanity through Him might be saved. (Jn.3:16-17) Jesus Christ said, "I am the way, the truth, and the life." He came to represent people before His Father, and to lead them away from the wrath that will try the world. He was speaking of His Church, and not physical buildings. (Jn.14:6)

Acts.1:8 is directly speaking to His Church who is His disciples, and He told the saints that they would receive power when the Spirit of God has come upon them, and they would be His witnesses from Jerusalem, Judea, Samaria and to the uttermost parts of the earth. He was talking to people who would carry on His mission of evangelism when He is gone from the earth. (Acts.2:47)

In Rom.12:3-4, 10, Paul was speaking to the Church, and he admonished them that they should offer their lives unto God as living sacrifice, breathing and walking in Christ. They were to be seen as living, and not dead sacrifice on the altar of the Lord. The worship and sacrifices of their lives are living, holy, and acceptable to God. This type of worship and sacrifices are precious unto God, and He is very pleased. They should be kindly affectionate to one another with brotherly love; in honor preferring one another. (v.10)

In their social lives together, they should do all things to the glory of God in eating, drinking and socializing. (1Cor.10:31-33) By so doing they will give none offense to the Jews, Gentiles or the Church of God. He gave himself as an example as he served our world of humanity, seeking the profit of many in order that they might be saved.

In 1Cor.12:12-26, Paul again here was talking to a flesh and blood Church, purchased by the blood of the Lamb of God. He said to them that they are one body, and had many members, and all the members of that one body, being many, are one body, even as Christ is One. He went on to say that through one Spirit, we are all baptized into one body, whether we are Jews or Gentiles, bond or free; and we have been made to drink into one Spirit. There is no "I" in team, and He was not speaking to bricks and mortal of a physical building.

The beginning of equating the living Church to where she meets is an abomination to the first century saints of God. The places that housed the Church are separate and distinct from the Church. We are spirit beings, but our bodies are not our spirits. We have a house or building called the body, and the spirit inside expresses itself through the body. That is the function of the place that the Church meets, for the worship of Christ and the Almighty God.

In 1Thes.4:17, Paul was addressing the Church, and he was giving her hope, that those who are alive will not precede the dead, but will be caught up with the Lord in the air after the dead are raised up in glory. We shall be caught up together, and we shall meet the Lord in the air. We will be with the Lord forever and ever.

Why would people say that they are going to the Church every Sunday? Can the Church go to the Church? No, a thousand times no. The Church goes to a place of worship, the place where we gather together for the purpose of praising and worshipping the Lord God and His Christ. The whole Church of Jesus Christ has bought into this lie of the enemy to focus the Church on the physical, instead of the spiritual. The word says; "Man shall not live on bread alone, but by every word that proceeds out the mouth of the living God". (Matt.4:4)

The Church must make a conscious effort not to demean herself, and use the designation of God to her truthfully. She must be properly designated in functioning on this terrestrial ball. She is the Bride of Christ, the Pillar and Ground of truth according to 1Tim.3:14-15. He says, "But if I tarry long, that you may know how you ought to behave yourselves in the House of God, which is the Church of the living God, the Pillar and Ground of truth.

The Church of living God cannot be a structure made with men's hands, but as she is truly, the Pillar and Ground of truth. The Head of the Church is Christ, and the Head of Christ is God, the Father. If the last two are spiritual, then the third must also be. The last two are not physical structures, then it follows that the Church cannot be of a physical structure, but of the

Spirit. They are divine in their nature. Therefore, the Church cannot be physical, but spiritual. Indeed, God within her is the Pillar and Ground of truth. (1Tim.3:15)

In 1Tim.5:1-3, Paul was addressing the Church, and in particular, the widows and the young women who have been widowed by the loss of their husbands. He was not talking to inanimate objects, but living, breathing and organic Church of flesh and bones. He told the Church that they ought to take into consideration widows who were widows indeed. He admonished the young women to get married, but only in the Lord.

In 1Cor.1:17, Paul was talking to the gainsayers who were once part of the saints. He said to them that Christ has not sent him to baptize, but to preach the Gospel. He maintained that he has been given the Spirit of God, and not the spirit of this world. He did not want the Gospel of Christ to be made of no effect through the wisdom of man.

God made man in His Image and after His Likeness, and man is like God, and not the other way around. People are the ones that Jesus Christ came for, and they are the ones made in the Image and Likeness of the Living God. Not the place of gathering where the Church meets for the worship of God during the week, either on Sundays or Saturdays.

In Heb.10:1ff, we have been sanctified through the offering of the body of Jesus Christ once and for all by the means of His eternal blood, on the mercy seat of God, Almighty. In v.19, we have boldness to enter into the most holy place by the blood of Jesus Christ. This is the new and living way that God has consecrated for us through the flesh of Jesus Christ. We are a redeemed people, and have been cleansed by His precious blood. And in v.25, he said that we should not forsake the assembling or coming together of the people of God, but we are to exhort one another: and so much the more, as we see the coming of Christ's day approaching.

People are the ones who are coming together, and not bricks, cement, nails and all the building materials that make the physical buildings. In 2Chro.7:14, God, Almighty said to His people; "If My people, who are called by My name, should humble themselves, and pray, and seek My face, and turn from their wicked ways; then will I hear from heaven. I will forgive their sins, and will heal their land." Just as the Church is people in the New Testament, even so was the Old Testament, not building, synagogue or temple, but those who were made in the Image and Likeness of the Living God.

In the dedication of the Temple of God built by Solomon, which his father David wanted to build for God, Solomon said, "Now therefore, let it please You to bless this house of your servant, that it may be before You forever: for You bless, O Lord, and it shall be blessed forever". (1Chro.17:1-27)

There is glory, honor and blessing upon the physical building, a place of worship, because of God's people are within it. God will bless it for the request of His people, and not without them. God will sanctify the Temple because of the people of God, and the presence of God can linger more than several years in it. We must be careful not to assign glory to the house, apart from the righteousness of God, and the people of God.

The Church is the House of God, the Church of the living God. He called His Church, the House of the living God, and not the building that houses the living organism. The Church is part and parcel of the Son, the Lord of His Church. The scripture for this is 1Tim.3:15b. We should have no question about the Church being an extension of the True Vine. (Jn.15:5)

The following scriptures confirmed the Church as a living organism: Heb.10:6 and 25; Col.1:17-20, 3:14-16; Eph.1:18-23, 2:19-20, 3:14-22 and 5:25-32.

Chapter Ten

THE FIRST HUNDRED YEARS OF HIS CHURCH

(WORKS, MINISTRY AND PEOPLE)

The word "Church" means "assembly or gathering". The first Church met in the homes of Christians to celebrate Jesus Christ and the forms this celebration took varies, but they were involved in praying, singing of hymns, spiritual songs, reading of OT Scriptures, sharing meals together, healing, words of exaltation, encouragement, the gifts of the Spirit and many other stuffs, orchestrated by the Spirit of God. The glory, honor and the Lordship of Jesus Christ were the central core of this community.

There were leaders of these House Churches and their names were mentioned in the scriptures, as well as the city where they were. Although little is known of them, they were remembered as early followers of Christ, who opened their homes for Christian fellowships or who led local groups of Christians in House Churches.

Training, education and mentorship are very important for an individual to take on the role of being a facilitator, moderator, coordinator or House Church leader, but it does not mean a paper qualification. Twelve men went to Christ's school and it did not involve paper qualification. These 12 men were with the Lord for three and half years. They were under authority before they could be in authority.

The Church in her first 100 years, met in the homes, public places and rooms that could contain her. The leaderships were pluralistic in nature, and no one single person was considered the leader. (Acts.13:1-3) They have leaders among them, and it was first among the equals. They functioned within the cities, and carried out their works under the Lordship of Jesus Christ.

The leaders were pastors, elders, apostles, evangelists, teachers and prophets, such as Peter, John, James, the apostles, Phoebe, Gaius, Aquila, Priscilla, Philemon, Nympha, Philip, Barnabas, Saul, Simeon, Lucius, Manaen, Titus, Lydia, Timothy, John Mark and elders to mention a few. They met in different cities like Cenchreas, Corinth, Ephesus, Colossae, Laodicea, Caesarea, Antioch, Crete, Thyatira, Thessalonica, Philippi, Lystra, Jerusalem and others.

The office of the pastor like it is today, did not overcome the others offices. Pastors in the 21st century have become larger than life, and they occupied the position of the Lord, reserved for Him alone. Pastors, because they founded they inorganic church, claimed the ownership of the human built organization. Jesus Christ did not intend it to be so. The leaders of the world exercise authority over their subordinates, but with the Church, it shall not be so. (Matt.20:20-28)

The following scriptures do testifiy of them: Rom.16:1-2, 23ff, 1Cor.1:1-2, Acts.18:1ff, Rom.16:3ff, Philemon.1:2, Col.4:15, Acts.16:8, Titus.1:4-6, Acts.21:8, Acts.13:1-2, 1Thess.1:1ff, Acts.14:23, 1Tim.1:3, Acts.16:25-34, Acts.12:12-17 and others.

CHRIST LIKE
Christianity

Acts.7:44-50
Exo.38-40
Exo. 25:8-9
Exo. 38:21
Exo. 25:40
IKg.16:1-38
IKg.8:20
IIKg.3:1-17
Lk.1:32
Isa. 66:1-2
Matt.5:34ff
Deut.32:49
Josh.3:14
Josh.18:1
Josh.23:9-11
Josh.24:18
Psm.44:2ff
IISam.7:8ff, 1-16
Psm.132:1-5
Acts.7:1-16
IChro.17:1-14

The responsibility of building the Church was not given to man, and it was the prerogative of the Lord Jesus Christ, and the Spirit of God. (Matt.16:18) God called us not to build His Church, but to be witnesses unto Him around the world of His power, saving grace, love, mercy and compassion to the saints and sinners. No one born of woman can build the Church of God. In Acts.2:42-47, we have an example of how God is building His Church.

The Spirit of God empowered Peter to deliver a moving sermon, (word) and the result was three thousand souls were added to "The Way" The three thousand continued steadfastly in the apostles doctrine, fellowship, breaking of bread and in prayers. They have no problem in finding places, houses or homes to contain them. The word of God said they were breaking bread and fellowshipping in homes. Three thousand men and women were breaking bread and fellowshipping in homes. Amazing! The hand of the Lord was with them, and fear fell upon every soul outside "The Way".

They were together and had all things in common, selling their possessions and goods, and parting them to all the saints as they have need. They were in the Temple for the larger body, but in the houses with lesser group of 8-15. They were breaking bread from house to house, and eating meat with gladness and singleness of heart. The Spirit of God held them together and the apostles were simply coordinators over the household of God.

In Acts.4:4, the number of The Way was increased to 5,000, and the Spirit of God was in charge, not man. The political and religious leaders wanted to kill them, but God kept His hand upon their lives. (vv.17-21, 31-37, 5:17-25) They were threatened and let go, but God kept guiding them through the power of His Spirit.

CHURCHES IN THE CITIES

Millions of millions of House Churches will be in a city, and from the North, South, East and West. She will occupy a notable place of honor before God and a catalyst to the city, province and Nation in terms of its population and the way of life.

SIZABLE GOAL

Reality: We will start with 50, 100, 150, 200 and beyond in House Churches, and she will grow in strength, wisdom, power and might of the Lord.

SHEPHERD

God is the Shepherd of His flock and Jesus Christ is watching over all by the Spirit of God. Apostles, prophets, evangelists, pastors and teachers will flow according to the will of God.

PRIESTHOOD

Everyone who has met Jesus Christ and in love with Him and has come under His Lordship, having Him as the Lord, Redeemer and Savior of their lives, will come forward to honor His name.

GROUPS OF 2, OR 8-10

The city will have as its goal 8-10 or 10-15 meeting in houses just like the NT Church. The body will have the opportunity to excel in love, ministry, worship, spontaneity, prophecy, gifts of the spirit and much more.

NO BUILDING

There will be no building to maintain, no over head cost, no hydro bills, heating bills, repairs, paying salaries etc. The lowest number is 2 and the fuller number is 8-20 people in all. (Matt.18:20)

NO MONEY MATTER

The Church will have money to do what she has always wanted to do, and be able to reach out to the poor, the needy, the orphans, widows, fatherless, and take care of her own responsibilities.

INTERACTIONS

The Church will meet not just one or two times a week, but often in person, through telephone, through email, through letter writing, visits, in coffee shops and house meetings.

GOD'S GIFTS

This will create rumblings in the spiritual and physical worlds. The community, society and people will take notice of the Lord Christ and His Father, the Creator of all things. Winnipeg House Churches will become the organic NT Church. They will be patterned according to what prevailed in the first century Church. They will have no structures, buildings, cathedrals or super, mega buildings, and yet they will be in the thousands. The Lord said where two or three are gathered in His name, there He is in the midst of them. (Matt.18:19-20)

Houses or homes are the meeting places of the Organic Church, and it has no pastor in the contemporary sense, and yet there are the five folds ministry available in their midst. It does not have bills, and no paid pastors, assistant administrators, Sunday School workers, custodians, security men, office managers, secretaries and a whole lot of personnel.

They did not have overhead bills to worry about, neither did they pay for electricity, heating, plumbing, air-conditions and most of the things the modern churches spend money for. They did not pay tithes and yet more money proceeds out of them than the tithing mandated of the OT. They knew what Christ has done for them and the grace of generous, cheerful, joyful, abundant giving out-shines the OT Law of tithing.

We are here to glorify the Lord God, our Creator and live for Him by trusting Christ, the Redeemer, from hell and self. We are also to give to humanity from what we have. Give and it shall be given back to you. God will cause people to give back to you. (Lk.6:38)

The heart of the Lord is with people who are with Him in sincerity and honesty. If you seek the Lord, you will find Him and your joy will know no boundary. But if you think you can trick Him by pulling some wool over His eyes, you have pitched your tent with Satan, and your ruin will be great!

God knows you and where you are in this world. He knew the Eunuch of Ethiopia, the Minister of Finance under Candace, the Queen of Ethiopia. He knows your heart and the lies, corruption, deception, wickedness and the evil you do in secret places. If you ask Christ, He will satisfy your spiritual hunger! (Acts.8:26-39)

There are engineers, doctors, pharmacists, business tycoons, ministers in governments and thousands of fine minds in the Kingdom, but they buried their heads in the sand like an Ostrich, and cannot see that God is not about building, structures and mega cathedrals. Read the Book of Acts.

Saying the sinner's prayers and being baptized are moves towards Christ in God. They are the essence of your faith. But you have to do better than that for the human heart is evil and wicked above all things. Have a humble, transparent and open heart in sincerity, and the Spirit of God will make your heart His home.

Simon in Acts.8:9-24, received Jesus and was baptized, but he was in the gall of bitterness and iniquity. You may be exactly like Simon who confessed Jesus, but his heart was a million miles away from God. Blessed are the pure in heart for they shall see God. (Matt.5:8)

Chapter Eleven

BAD EGGS IN HIS CHURCH

(ROBBERS AND THEIVES)
(JAZEBELS, NICOLAITANS, BALAAMS)
JN.10:10, REV.2:9

These following behaviors are some of the practices of the Church of Jesus Christ in the 21st Century in our world today. Do these describe you or someone you may know?

Rev. Bodzo Koyo is the pastor of a local Church in Nowhere City. He receives a salary from this Church, and yet has a personal ministry by name: Bodzo Koyo Ministries. It is an individual ministry, and he is the only one who is accountable for it. Did you see apostle Paul doing this in the first Century Church?

Jesus Christ never had a ministry named after Him. He came as the servant of God, and He did what He heard and saw His Father doing. (Jn.5:19, 30) Paul and Barnabas were sent by the Spirit and as well as the Church. (Acts.13) They never had Paul and Barnabas Ministries. In today's world, there are ministers of Churches who have ministries after their names. These ministers have personal ministries after their names, and still collect salaries from the Churches.

Some of the ministers of these Churches pay money to obtain Doctorate Degrees from a body of Institutions, and they are accredited for it. They give them the office of a Bishop, Arch Bishop, Arch-Apostles, Apostles, Arch-Deacons, Arch-Elders and more. They elevate these honorific titles above the Five-Fold Ministries that Jesus Christ appointed for His Church.

Some saints are even displeased if the titles of Dr. Apostle, Arch-Bishop, Bishop, Arch-Apostle and Arch-Deacon do not prefix their names. There are bodies in Christendom who give accreditation and recognition to these titles. If you can pay for the titles of a Doctor, Bishop, Apostle, Arch Bishop and Arch Apostle on this planet, then you can have it. It is a question of how deep is your pocket.

Peter, James, John, Andrew and all the disciples of the Lord before they were sent to the world, would cringe at today's Church. The practices are foreign to them, and the mandate they received from the Lord of the Church. They never saw it in their Lord and Master, the Owner of the Church. The Scriptures call the Lord Jesus Christ, "The Apostle and High Priest of our profession or confession, and also the Shepherd and Bishop of our souls." (Heb.3:1, 1Pet.2:25)

An apostle is a sent one like John Zacharias, Jesus Christ, and by implication, the first twelve disciples of Christ. He sent them to the world to continue where He had stopped. Jesus Christ was sent by God from heaven to the earth. John the Baptist was sent by God from heaven to the earth. When you come back from your mission, you are just like the rest of us. You may be a deacon, an elder, a pastor, an evangelist or a prophet before you were sent.

A bishop is a shepherd, an elder or a pastor who provides spiritual care for the people under Christ among other things. Christ is the Chief Shepherd under whom they serve God. It is not a huge or mighty title by which you may be called. The power is not in the name, but in God.

These are some scriptures referring to us as the Building of God in Christ: "Who His own self bare our sins in His own body on the tree, that we, being dead to sins, should live unto righteousness: by whose stripes you were healed. For you were a sheep going astray; but are now returned to the Shepherd and Bishop of your souls. Wherefore, holy brethren, partakers of the heavenly calling, consider the Apostle and High Priest of our profession, declaration or confession, Christ Jesus; who was faithful to Him that appointed Him." (1Pet.2:25, Heb.3:1-2) Let us not crack heads because of the proliferation of titles in our world today.

The words simply mean a servant in charge of His Church under Him. That is what an elder, a bishop, an overseer or a pastor means. Let us not jump the hoop because of names and titles. If the Lord sends you, then you are an apostle, but when you come back from where He has sent you, don't impose the title or office on yourself towards the people. Shepherd, pastor that serve as a bishop under His congregation, and serve Him faithfully.

As for the place where the Church meets, the Lord places more emphasis on the hearts of the worshippers than the place where they meet. It does not matter to Him at all. If His Church meets in a mega church building, cathedral or a thatched hut, God considers the spirits of His people whether they tremble at His Word or disobey it.

The saints in His Church, who practice these systems of the world, will face the Master and Owner of the Church one of these days. Millions and billions of dollars have been taken from the people of God to build their own empires, kingdoms and businesses. They have made a name for themselves, instead of God making their names great upon the earth. These so called saints are reliving Gen.11, and will not submit to the rule of God, and allow Him to make them great as He did to Abraham in Gen.12.

We have come to value names, honors, titles and accolades of men more than the words of God and of His Spirit. We have not cherished what He has given to us His children. If you are not a Doctor, Bishop, Apostle and Arch-Bishop, and have no clout with men, the Church will not recognize you, even if you are a child of God.

We measure people's standard with God according to the size of their church buildings, and the number of their congregations. Do we fear and tremble at His word, or prefer to have thousand of people in our congregation who come to fill our buildings, a place designated for the worship of our God?

The author believes that evangelism can be carried out with the body of believers in a local Church, and ministers of God do not have to separate it from His Church. The evangelism and outreaches performed by the ministers of the Church can be under the same umbrella of the Church, oversees by the Lord, her Owner. There is no need for secrecy or the fear that someone in the board will discover some anomalies in the books. Fear, disbelief and the lack of trust lead men of God to sidetrack His Church to begin something that has shady and misgiving prospect.

The work of God can be done in a transparent environment, and beyond elements of doubt and mistrust. God is not a loner, and His people should not entertain any form of mistrust. The minister who serves in a local church should declare his earning of his outreaches to the local Church that is responsible for his wages. He ought to give an account of his personal ministry to the people of God. There is no personal ministry in the body of Christ, because He never passed on to us this act of robbing His Church when He was leaving us for His Father.

Jesus Christ drove the worshippers from the Temple of God, because they have abused and misrepresented the Lord. Instead of them encouraging the maim, the blind, the cripple and others to come and find relief in the Temple, they turned it to a commercial center, where selling and buying came above getting the needs of the common people met. They have made the House of God a den of thieves and a rendezvous where evil are hatched. The Holy Spirit then left the Temple when Christ blood atoned for humanity. (Matt.27:50-51)

The people of God are no longer content or satisfied with what Christ had given to His Church in Eph.4:11 and 1Cor.12:28. We crave better titles than what has been given to us in order to face the challenges of our planet. God is all and in all, and His Son, Jesus Christ is above all except His Father. He is the Lord of the Sabbath and the Temple, and He is the head of man, just as the man is the head of the woman. (1Cor.11:3)

In Matt.23:13-22 and 12:3-8, Jesus Christ made certain utterances that are worth looking into. The political and religious leaders of the Jews were more into the letters of the Law than its spirit.

They maintained that you can swear by the Temple, and God will not contend with you, but if you swear by the gold in the Temple, you will be touching the apple of the eye of God. God is the Head of all things, both animate and inanimate. He is the Head of Christ, and Christ is the Head of man, and man is the head of the woman. (1Cor.11:3) In seeing things that have life and spirit in them, both God and His Christ are greater than all.

Christ, who has both seen and heard from His Father, did not make God a task Master, but one who is benevolent, and cares deeply for His creation. How did we ever get here? We have made a monster of the things of God, and created supper high hierarchy amongst the people of God that He has not made. Let us return to the simple, but easy and meek Lord, in order to function as the people of God.

Jesus Christ said that the Jews were misleading the people. He said, "You fools and blind: for which is greater, the gift, or the altar that sanctifies the gift? Whoso therefore shall swear by the altar, swear by it, and by all things thereon. And whoso ever shall swear by the Temple, swear by it, and by Him that dwells therein. And he that swears by heaven, swears by the throne of God, and by Him that seats thereon."

In other words, the building is not greater than the people of God, who meet there to worship God. God is the ultimate Being, the un-created Creator and the un-beginning Beginner. He is the greatest of all, and there is nothing close to Him in splendor and greatness. When the Church comes together to worship God, the house where she meets is inferior to the Church, because Christ lives in them, and He is the hope of glory. The Church should never ascribe worth to a physical building apart from the Christ in her. The Organism is far more important than the organization. We are the dwelling place of God, and His presence remains and dwells in and among us all.

Ministers of God, with giant cathedrals and mega buildings, who have thousands of people that attend services every Sunday with a mindset of the world, are playing games with the Satan, the enemy. Some of them had met with Belial, the prince of demons, and they entered into an agreement with Satan. The conclusion of that agreement is the production of three cows that are buried alive under the altar in the sanctuary. As the cows decays and produce maggots, souls will begin to pour into the church building. The numbers of maggots will equal the number of the congregation. The supposed ministers of God are playing with fire, and it will burn them to ashes at the end of their days.

There are these types of congregations in the 21st century across the globe: North, South, East and West. These ministers are so desperate, because of the pressure of the world to produce a mega congregation. They are driven to the enemy to assist them in achieving what God has not sanctioned. These are the churches of Satan, camouflaging as the Church of God. (Read Rev.2:9) In His address to them, He said: "I know your works, and tribulation, and poverty, (but you are rich) and I know the blasphemy of them who say they are Jews, and are not, but they are the Church of Satan". (vv.9-10)

As it were, some of us have negated the word of God for our traditions, and have set up all kinds of offices, titles and hierarchy for ourselves, thereby negating and contradicting the word of God. The Christian is trying to live like a Jew, and the Jew is trying to live like the Christian. Paul addressed this issue in Gal.2:12 and the Council in Jerusalem addressed it too, when some Jews came to Antioch and said that the saints must be circumcised. Acts.15:1, 22-29 was the answer of the Church, the Apostles and the Elders to resolve this problem.

Moses, Joshua, Elijah, Ezekiel, Jeremiah, Isaiah, David and including all the saints of the Old and New Testaments in the first century did not practice these forms of double dipping in the ministry of the Lord committed to their care. No one has a ministry, and we are an extension of His Ministry here on earth. We are mandated to carry on where Christ has end, and we are to continue His Ministry.

Chapter Twelve

THE CHURCH AS SHE WAS AND LIVED

The standard response we generally give, is to try and briefly explain our understanding of what Scripture teaches about the Church, the Bride of Christ.

Rom.16:5, 1Cor.16:19, Col.4:15 and Phil.2 describe Church as meeting in homes. This was the standard. It is the norm. Small groups of the saints meeting in homes, allow, not only them, but us, to minister one to another. Special church buildings, programs, services, and crowds did not show up on the scene until several hundred years late. Eph.2:19 teaches that, we are "fellow citizens with the saints, and are of God's household…" We are truly families. Families take care of each other. They watch out for each other, and are committed to the Lord and the Body.

Acts.2:42 teaches that continuously, the Church engaged in at least four primary activities: 1) Devoting themselves to the apostles' teaching, 2) To fellowship, 3) To the breaking of bread, and 4) To prayer.

ICor.14:26 describes what they were instructed to do, when they gathered: "When you assemble, each one has a psalm, has a teaching, has a revelation, has a tongue, has an interpretation. Let all things be done for edification." Everyone is encouraged to participate and bring something of edification to the gathering. Church is not a spectator sport where only a few perform and the rest are spectators.

Heb.10:24-25 teaches us the reason for gathering, "and let us consider how to stimulate one another to love and good deeds, not forsaking our own assembling together, as is the habit of some, but encouraging one another; and all the more as you see the day drawing near." The main reasons why we are admonished to gather are to: 1) Stimulate one another to love and good deeds. 2) Encourage one another. If our gatherings do not encourage and motivate us to truly love one another and perform good deeds, then something is out of line and needs to be corrected.

There are many other passages that relate to the who, what, when, where, and why of the Church. A few that amplify and describe the above in greater detail are ICor.11-12-13-14, IPet.2, Acts.2:42-47, and ITim.3.

"If your brother sins against you, go and tell him his fault, between you and him alone. If he listens to you, you have gained your brother. But if he does not listen, take one or two more with you, so that they may witness the matter. If he refuses to listen to them, tell it to the Church. And if he refuses to listen even to the Church, let him be to you as a Gentile and a tax collector. Truly, I say to you, whatever you bind on earth, shall be bound in heaven, and whatever you loose on earth, shall be loosed in heaven. Again I say unto you, if two of you shall agree on earth about anything they shall ask, it shall be granted them by my Father in heaven. For where two or three are gathered together in my name, there am I among them." (Matt.18:15-20)

And Jesus returned in the power of the Spirit to Galilee, and the report about him went out through all the surrounding country.

And he taught in their synagogues, being glorified by all.

And he came to Nazareth, where he had been brought up. And as was his custom, he went to the synagogue on the Sabbath day, and he stood up to read. (Lk.4:14-16)

So those who received his word were baptized, and there were added that day about three thousand souls. (Acts.2:41) So we, though many, are one body in Christ, and individual members of one another. (Rom.12:5) But in the following instructions, I do not commend you, because when you come together, it is not for the better, but for the worse. For, in the first place, when you come together as a Church, I hear that there are divisions among you. And I believe it in part, 1Cor.11:17-18.

For just as the body is one and has many members, and all the members of the body, though many, are one body, so it is with Christ. For in one Spirit, we were all baptized into one body—Jews or Greeks, slaves or free—and all were made to drink of one Spirit.

For the body does not consist of one member, but of many. If the foot should say, "Because I am not a hand, I do not belong to the body," that would not make it any less a part of the body. And if the ear should say, "Because I am not an eye, I do not belong to the body," that would not make it any less a part of the body. If the whole body were an eye, where would be the sense of hearing? If the whole body were an ear, where would be the sense of smell? But as it is, God arranged the members in the body, each one of them, as he choses. If all were a single member, where would the body be? As it is, there are many parts, yet one body.

The eye cannot say to the hand, "I have no need of you," nor again the head to the feet, "I have no need of you." On the contrary, the parts of the body that seem to be weaker are indispensable, and on those parts of the body that we think less honorable, we bestow the greater honor, and our un-presentable parts are treated with greater modesty, which our more presentable parts do not require. But God has so composed the body, giving greater honor to the part that lacked it, that there may be no division in the body, but that the members may have the same care for one another. If one member suffers, all suffer together; if one member is honored, all rejoice together.

Now you are the body of Christ and individually members of it. (1Cor.12:12-27) I thank God that I speak in tongues more than all of you. Nevertheless, in Church, I would rather speak five words with my mind in order to instruct others, than ten thousand words in tongue

Brothers, do not be children in your thinking. Be infants in evil, but in your thinking, be mature. In the Law it is written, "By people of strange tongues and by the lips of foreigners will I speak to this people, and even then, they will not listen to me, says the Lord." Thus tongues are a sign, not for believers, but for unbelievers, while prophecy is a sign, not for unbelievers, but for believers. If therefore, the whole Church comes together and all speak in tongues, and outsiders or unbelievers enter, will they not say that you are out of your minds? But if all prophesy, and an unbeliever or outsider enters, he is convicted by all, he is called to account by all, the secrets of his heart are disclosed, and so, falling on his face, he will worship God and declare that God is really among you. (1Cor.14:18-25)

Wives, submit to your own husbands, as to the Lord. For the husband is the head of the wife, even as Christ is the head of the Church, his body, and is himself its Savior. Now as the Church submits to Christ, so also wives should submit, in everything to their husbands.

Husbands, love your wives, as Christ loved the Church and gave himself up for her, that he might sanctify her, having cleansed her by the washing of water with the word, so that he might present the Church to himself in splendor, without spot or wrinkle or any such thing, that she might be holy and without blemish. In the same way husbands should love their wives as their own bodies. He who loves his wife, loves himself.

For no one ever hated his own flesh, but nourishes and cherishes it, just as Christ does the Church, because we are members of his body. "Therefore a man shall leave his father and mother and hold fast to his wife, and the two shall become one flesh." This mystery is profound, and I am saying that it refers to Christ and the Church. However, let each one of you love his wife as himself, and let the wife see that she respects her husband. (Eph.5:22-33)

And He is the head of the body, the Church. He is the beginning, the firstborn from the dead, that in everything, he might be preeminent. (Col.1:18) For he who sanctifies and those who are sanctified, all have one source. That is why he is not ashamed to call them brothers, saying, "I will tell of your name to my brothers; in the midst of the congregation, I will sing your praise." (Heb.2:11-12)

And let us consider how to stir up one another to love and good works, not neglecting to meet together, as is the habit of some, but encouraging one another, and all the more as you see the day drawing near. (Heb.10:24-25) My brothers, show no partiality as you hold the faith in our Lord Jesus Christ, the Lord of glory. For if a man wearing a gold ring and fine clothing comes into your assembly, and a poor man in shabby clothing also comes in, and if you pay attention to the one who wears the fine clothing and say, "You sit here in a good place," while you say to the poor man, "You stand over there," or, "Sit down at my feet," have you not then made distinctions among yourselves and become judges with evil thoughts? (Jms.2:1-4)

Chapter Thirteen

THE SCRIPTURES AND THE CHURCH

(WHAT THE SCRIPTURES SAY ABOUT THE CHURCH)

Eph.1:16-22. "I Cease not to give thanks for you, making mention of you in my prayers. That the God of our Lord Jesus Christ, the Father of glory, may give unto you the spirit of wisdom and revelation in the knowledge of Him: The eyes of your understanding being enlightened; that you may know what is the hope of His calling, and what the riches of the glory of His inheritance in the saints, and what is the exceeding greatness of His power to us-ward who believe, according to the working of His mighty power, which He wrought in Christ, when He raised Him from the dead, and set Him at His own right hand in the heavenly places, far above all principality, and power, and might, and dominion, and every name that is named, not only in this world, but also in that which is to come: and hath put all things under His feet, and gave Him to be the head over all things to the Church, which is His body, the fullness of Him that fills all in all.

Eph.2:10-22. For we are his workmanship, created in Christ Jesus unto good works, which God hath before ordained that we should walk in them. Wherefore remember, that ye being in time past Gentiles in the flesh, who are called un-circumcision by that which is called the Circumcision in the flesh made by hands; that at that time ye were without Christ, being aliens from the commonwealth of Israel, and strangers from the covenants of promise, having no hope, and without God in the world, but now in Christ Jesus, you who sometimes were far off are made nigh by the blood of Christ.

For He is our peace, who hath made both one, and has broken down the middle wall of partition between us; having abolished in His flesh the enmity, even the law of commandments contained in ordinances; for to make in Himself of twain one new man, so making peace; and that He might reconcile both unto God in one body by the cross, having slain the enmity thereby: and came and preached peace to you which were afar off, and to them that were nigh. For through Him we both have access by one Spirit unto the Father.

Now therefore you are no more strangers and foreigners, but fellow citizens with the saints, and of the household of God, and are built upon the foundation of the apostles and prophets, Jesus Christ Himself being the chief corner stone. In whom all the building fitly framed together grows unto an holy temple in the Lord. In whom ye also are built together for an habitation of God through the Spirit.

Eph.3:14-21. For this cause I bow my knees unto the Father of our Lord Jesus Christ, of whom the whole family in heaven and earth is named. That He would grant you, according to the riches of his glory, to be strengthened with might by His Spirit in the inner man. That Christ may dwell in your hearts by faith; that ye, being rooted and grounded in love, may be able to comprehend with all saints what is the breadth, and length, and depth, and height, and to know the love of Christ, which passes knowledge, that you might be filled with all the fullness of God. Now unto him that is able to do exceeding abundantly above all that we ask or think, according to the power that works in us.

Unto him be glory in the Church by Christ Jesus throughout

all ages, world without end. Amen! Matt.16:17-19. And Jesus answered and said unto him, Blessed are you, Simon Barjona: for flesh and blood has not revealed it unto you, but my Father which is in heaven. And I say also unto thee, that you are Peter, and upon this rock I will build My Church; and the gates of hell shall not prevail against it. And I will give unto you the keys of the kingdom of heaven: and whatsoever you shall bind on earth shall be bound in heaven: and whatsoever you shall loose on earth shall be loosed in heaven.

Acts.15:22-29. Then pleased it the apostles and elders with the whole Church, to send chosen men of their own company to Antioch with Paul and Barnabas; namely, Judas surnamed Barsabas and Silas, chief men among the brethren. And they wrote letters by them after this manner: "The apostles and elders and brethren send greeting unto the brethren which are of the Gentiles in Antioch and Syria and Cilicia.

Forasmuch as we have heard, that certain which went out from us have troubled you with words, subverting your souls, saying, you must be circumcised, and keep the law: to whom we gave no such commandment. It seemed good unto us, being assembled with one accord, to send chosen men unto you with our beloved Barnabas and Paul. These men have hazarded their lives for the name of our Lord Jesus Christ. We have sent therefore, Judas and Silas, who shall also tell you the same things by mouth. For it seemed good to the Holy Ghost, and to us, to lay upon you no greater burden than these necessary things. That you abstain from meats offered to idols, and from blood, and from things strangled, and from fornication: from which if you keep yourselves, you shall do well. Fare ye well.

Heb.12:22-24. But you are come unto mount Zion, and unto the city of the living God, the heavenly Jerusalem, and to an innumerable company of angels, to the general assembly and Church of the firstborn, which are written in heaven, and to God the Judge of all, and to the spirits of just men made perfect, and to Jesus the mediator of the new covenant, and to the blood of sprinkling, that speaks better things than that of Abel.

Heb.12:1-21. Wherefore seeing we also are compassed about with so great a cloud of witnesses, let us lay aside every weight, and the sin which does so easily beset us, and let us run with patience the race that is set before us, looking unto Jesus the author and finisher of our faith; who for the joy that was set before Him endured the cross, despising the shame, and is set down at the right hand of the throne of God.

For consider Him that endured such contradiction of sinners against Himself, lest you be wearied and faint in your minds. You have not yet resisted unto blood, striving against sin. And you have forgotten the exhortation which speaks unto you as unto children, My son, despise not the chastening of the Lord, nor faint when you are rebuked of Him: for whom the Lord loves He chastens, and scourges every son whom he receives.

If you endure chastening, God deals with you as with sons; for what son is he whom the father chastens not? But if you are without chastisement, whereof all are partakers, then are you bastards, and not sons. Furthermore we have had fathers of our flesh who corrected us, and we gave them reverence: shall we not much rather be in subjection unto the Father of spirits, and live? For they verily for a few days chastened us after their own pleasure; but He for our profit, that we might be partakers of his holiness.

Now no chastening for the present seems to be joyous, but grievous: nevertheless afterward it yields the peaceable fruit of righteousness unto them who are exercised thereby. Wherefore lift up the hands that hang down, and the feeble knees; and make straight paths for your feet, lest that which is lame be turned out of the way; but let it rather be healed. Follow peace with all men, and holiness, without which no man shall see the Lord, looking diligently lest any man fail of the grace of God;

lest any root of bitterness springing up trouble you, and thereby many be defiled; Lest there be any fornicator or profane person as Esau, who for one morsel of meat sold his birthright.

You know how that afterward, when he would have inherited the blessing, he was rejected: for he found no place of repentance, though he sought it carefully with tears. For you are not come unto the mount that might be touched, and that burned with fire, nor unto blackness, and darkness, and tempest, and the sound of a trumpet, and the voice of words; which voice they that heard entreated that the word should not be spoken to them any more. For they could not endure that which was commanded, and if so much as a beast touches the mountain, it shall be stoned, or thrust through with a dart. And so terrible was the sight, that Moses said, I exceedingly fear and quake.

Eph.1:22, 2:10-22; Eph.4:24;
2Cor.5:17; Gal.2:21-22;
2Cor.5:15-21; 1Cor.10:4; Col.1:18

The Church cannot send anyone into the Mission Field. If she sends anyone, it will never be by the approval and consent of God. God sends before the Church approves in keeping with the will and purposes of God. Jesus Christ saw the actions and heard the words of His Father before He ever did anything on the earth.

Jesus Christ, John, the Baptist, the Apostles and the Prophets of God had to be sent first by God, and the Church must recognize what God has sanctioned. Moses was sent by God to the Hebrews in Egypt. (Exo.3:10) John was sent by God to the Israelites to be His Son's forerunner in preparation for the redemption of humanity. (Jn.1:6) Jesus Christ was sent by His Father to humanity to be the Savior of the world. (Jn.3:16) The apostles, Barnabas and Saul were sent by the Spirit of God to the Gentile world. (Acts.13:2-3) The scriptures say, "How can they preach unless they are sent?" (Rom.10:15)

God is the Maker, Owner and Creator of the 7.2 billion souls that live on earth today. We did not create ourselves, and we belong to God, the un-created Creator and the un-beginning Beginner. His are the Kingdom, the glory, the honor and the majesty. He owns the earth and the fullness thereof including mankind. He is the Boss and Big Kahuna of all from eternity past, present and future. He is the almighty God, and the Possessor of heaven and earth.

If we are sent from man without the previous approval from the Lord, we have no backing from heaven. Many have gone without Him sending them to go into the parts of the world. They were mostly subjected to the constant attack and the confrontation of the evil one.

God is the Owner of the people, and they numbered into 7.2 billion souls. The devil wants us to go in the power and authority of humanity, but such misguided venture is met with disasters and calamity. The power of the Holy Spirit should precede the missionaries, apostles, evangelists, prophets, teachers and pastors who must go to home and foreign lands to preach the Gospel.

Just because the Christ says, "Go Ye" does not mean go now. We must go, but we wait for the green light from the Lord of the harvest. We must seek His face in prayers, intercession and supplications if we want to be successful in working for the Lord. We must hear a fresh word from heaven before we proceed. He wants to go ahead of us, and we should not live Him behind. If we do the works of God by His instructions, ways and methods, His blessings will be upon us abundantly. There was no prophets who presumed upon the Lord in the OT when He has not sent them, neither has spoken to them. No ambassador goes from his home country without the backing of the government who is sending him.

Chapter Fourteen

ELDERS & BISHOPS ARE THE SAME

(1 TIM.3:1-13, TITUS.1:1-8, ACTS.14:23)

The word elder and bishop are directly connected to deacons and deaconesses. The scriptures used them in the same line, and they meant the servants of the Church like those in Acts.6 who were serving tables.

The word bishop has been flogged, abused, and torn into pieces to gain undue advantages over the people of God for popularity, power and wealth. God is not in it.

Strong's Concordance derived the meaning of these words from the reigning ecclesiastical government of the third to twenty-first centuries. Church leaders have removed this word from the Spirit's intention given by Paul, the Apostle. It has been wrenched from the general function of the Church, and has been given high and unparalleled position in our world today. The present day meaning of the word "bishop" is different from Paul's understanding of it by the Spirit of God.

In the Spirit's mind, and the mind of the Paul, it means a caregiver, leader, pastor or an elder. And from vv.2-6 of 1Tim.3, it gave us the functions of a bishop who is also an elder. The next office is lower than a bishop or elder, and this is a deacon/

deaconess. (v.8) He gave almost the same identical qualification to the one who desires the office of a deacon. Paul placed the deacons and bishops on the same threshold with the latter slightly higher than the former.

The word of God says, "The less is blessed of the better". (Heb.7:7) By that it means that the less is ordained by the greater, but in today's world, we say, "the greater is blessed by the less." Those who ordained elders and bishops like Gaius, Titus, Timothy and others are greater than the ones they appointed or ordained as bishops and elders according to the word of God. How can an elder or bishop be greater and higher than the office of the apostle, prophet, teacher, evangelist and pastor? Something is wrong with the theology of the modern man.

The one who blesses is always greater than the one who is blessed. If someone ordains you into a fraternity, he is greater than you. The one ordained could not be greater than the one who ordains him. Even so, the Timothies, the Tituses and Gaiuses of this world are greater than the people they have ordained. Timothy ordained the men in the fellowships around where Paul had sent him. Titus also ordained men where Paul sent him to as well. (Titus.1:5; Acts.14:23)

From the third to the twenty-first centuries, the Church Leaders are setting or pitching Paul against Jesus Christ, and are now saying this office of a bishop is higher than of a pastor, evangelist, teacher and probably the prophet and apostle. Jesus Christ gave us the Five-Fold Ministry of apostle, prophet, teacher, evangelist and pastor, and a bishop or deacon is not listed in it. We have elevated the word bishop above what it is meant to be.

There is no place in the Scriptures that Paul, Gaius, Timothy, Titus and others are called arch-apostles, arch-bishops, bishops and other honorific titles. It is misleading to designate ministers of the Gospel with titles that Christ never gave to them.

Going with the mentality of the leaders of the Church today, the bishops they ordained must be greater than those who ordained them into the ministry. (1Tim.3 and Titus.1)

This is not correct, and it is not the will of God to be so preoccupied with titles and offices in the Church. The hierarchy of the denominational Churches had sold the saints a bunch of hoopla in the elevation of the office of a bishop to a height above that of an apostle.

These Church Leaders have created for themselves positions that no one can touch, and not even God can touch them. They have also created different uniforms and purple garments that God did not call for. They have formed the College of Bishops, and moved one step next to their "god", the Pope. There are primarily for powers, money control and domination of the people of God.

In Titus, Paul wrote to his son Titus in the common faith. He said that he, Paul left him in Crete to set in order the things that are wanting or lacking, and to ordain elders/bishops in every city as he had appointed him. (Titus.1:5) Then he enumerated the qualification and functioning of the office of an elder. (v.6)

AN ELDER/BISHOP MUST BE:

1. Blameless
2. A one woman husband
3. Must have faithful children not accused of unruly behavior.

Then he changed the word elder for bishop, and continued his qualifications of an elder.

1. He repeated the word: Blameless. (v.7) Being steward of God.
2. Not self-willed, a one-way person, my way or the high way.

3. Not easily angered
4. Not given to wine
5. No striker. One who easily resort to fighting with his feast
6. Not a covetous person in terms of money. Filthy lucre.
7. Be a lover of hospitality. Willing to entertain strangers. (v.8)
8. A lover of good people.
9. Sober, just, holy and temperate.
10. Holding fast the faithful word as he has been taught, that he may be able by sound doctrine both to exhort and convince the gainsayers.

It is interesting that the word elder and bishop are interchangeable, and one can substitute either and it will mean the same. Paul's meaning is not what the bishops of this world and the College of Bishops have in mind for the Twenty First Century. Read the scriptures for yourselves in 1Tim.3:1-8, and Titus.1:1-9. Read them carefully and slowly. The total and collective role of a Bishop, Arch Bishop, Apostle, Arch Deacons and all the top offices and titles in the Church are for power, money, greed and the domination of the people of God.

A bishop is simply an elder, not necessarily an old person. An old person that has been long time in serving God can be called an elder, but not in this sense of a bishop or elder. An elder or a bishop is a little higher than a deacon or deaconess. They are just people who are serving and taking care of the flock of God, just like a pastor operating under the leadership role of the first amongst the equals.

How was it that the Christendom made such a big deal with these names and titles? In what year did honorific titles and names begin? It was in the 2nd century in which all hell broke loose upon the Church, and men were called all kinds of names. Jesus Christ did not call them the apostles that preceded them such names and titles.

Chapter Fifteen

FIVE FOLD MINISTRIES GIVEN TO THE CHURCH

(DEACONS, ELDERS AND BISHOPS ARE EXCLUDED)
(ICOR.12:27-31 & EPH.4:8-16)

The God-Head has functions, effects, administrations, offices, gifts, services and ministries that they are responsible for and it does not hinder their individuality or corporate roles.

The Ministry Gifts of people and the gifts of the Spirit work and operate hand in hand and without one the other is redundant. We need men and women, the gifts of Christ to the Church and even so we need the power and the anointing of the Holy Spirit in men and women to mature the Church and bring her to a place of authority here on earth. (Eph.4:11-12) What are reasons why the Church is so timid and backward when it comes to the Five Fold Ministries, the gifts of people to His Church? In the place that the Scripture mentioned apostles and prophets, is the same place that it mentioned pastors, teachers and evangelists. We cannot take one and leave the other because we don't like it or it will generate too much controversy. May be because we thought that the other "people gifts" like apostles and prophets are obsolete and we do not need them in our days and generation.

If ever there was an era where we need these gifts of apostles, prophets, teachers, evangelists and pastors, it is in this era and generation. Evil is exploding with an amazing rapidity and human knowledge, science, technology, computer, medical field, invention and creativity are riding on its back. So we need the Ministry Gifts and the Gifts of the Holy Spirit to help us fulfill the mandate of the Lord as we gather mankind unto Him for His glory and honor. We need Him and God's Spirit to show us what we cannot know of ourselves and by ourselves.

We need to know the minds of governors, prime ministers, presidents, ministers and governments. We need to know the things that are discussed in the chambers and bedrooms of the men and women who control this world of our Father. We need to know the hearts and secrets of kings and queens behind the walls of their homes and thousands of miles away. These are what the Spirit of God delights in doing and telling the servants of God for the purpose of gathering unto Him the kingdoms of this world and all humanity. (Eph.4:11-12) The Lord Jesus Christ is so excited to show these things to His servants in order to prove the foolishness of the wisdom of this world.

In every local Church, God has ordained the Five-fold Ministries in them and it is a question of recognizing the authority that the Lord has placed in His Church. We have apostles, prophets, teachers, pastors and evangelists amongst us. We have to promote, create the awareness, be bold in talking about them and make the topics a house-hold issue. There are people among us that the Lord wants to send to the nations. There are people in our fellowshaips that He wants to send forth as evangelists. There are people that He wants to use as prophets and teachers. There are people that He wants to use as pastors.

All these people gifts are found within a local Church and wherever they go, they will always come back to the home Church to tell or recount their stories and experiences. They will be refreshed, recuperated, energized, encouraged and blessed by the Church before they go out again. This is what the Lord wants to do for His Church and what a power-house the

Church will be if she functions this way.

Why do we not promote, encourage and teach these truths? Why have we settled for the offices of the pastors, evangelists and teachers and neglected the offices of the apostles and prophets? Was this the Lord's doing or the enemy's? Will God give us five things and then say we can only claim three of them? Is the controversy coming from the camp of Satan to weaken our resolve about what the Lord said is ours? Let's talk about them and shout it on the mountains till the whole world knows and keenly aware of it. The Five-fold Ministries and the Gifts of the Spirit are for us today and we have them amongst us.

Christ and the Spirit of God are not in competition with each other and He is part and parcel of the Father who manages all the operations in heaven and earth. The Father sent the Son and the Son sent the Holy Spirit even as He requested the Spirit from His Father. Christ gives the gifts of men and women, and the Spirit of God gives both men and women God's gifts to encourage, bless and mature the Church till Jesus Christ returns. (Eph.4:11-13)

The Old Testament had prophets, teachers, pastors and probably evangelists, but it never mentioned apostles. It is uniquely a New Testament revelation to ordain men as His apostles who would go with the Gospel message to the ends of the world according to the mandate of the Lord. The gifts of the Holy Spirit are present in both dispensations. People were raised from the dead, lepers were cleansed, a whole army captured supernaturally, people were fed through divine power and grace, others received healing miracles from heaven divinely.

The seas were parted and there were miracles galore all over in both Testaments. But these are the generations that will usher in the beginning of the millennium and the coming of the Prince of Peace. Therefore, we need the Ministry Gifts of Christ and the anointing of the Holy Spirit as never before in this present civilization in which the door of the mercy of Lord has been opened indefinitely for the ingathering of whosoever wills.

The gifts of the Spirit are the gifts of God and they are nine representing all that He has for us, and the world of angels and men. They are not exhaustive and God has not limited Himself as in the covenant He made with Noah when He set the rainbow in the skies that He would not destroy the world with water as He did before. God can do any and every thing and no one can question His Power. In the gifts of the Spirit, the Word of God enumerated nine and the manifestations are solely the prerogatives of the Spirit of God. The system is divided into three areas and the gifts of the Spirit are divided into three groups of three. In this system, we have the first one which are the diversities of Gifts and they are manned by God's Spirit. Secondly, we have the differences of administrations that are manned by the Lord Jesus Christ. The third one are the diversities of operations and these are the prerogative of the Father, who is the Great "I AM".

The nine gifts of the Spirit are further divided into groups of three. First we have the gifts that reveal or show something. Secondly, we have the gifts that do something and are the gifts of power. And finally, we have the gifts that say something and they are the gifts of utterance. The gifts of Power are the working of miracles, the gifts of healing and faith. The gifts of Speech or Utterance are prophecy, divers kinds of tongues and the interpretation of tongues. The gifts of Revelation or Disclosure are the word of wisdom, the word of knowledge and the distinguishing of spirits.

The Word of God did not categorize them in that order, however, they function along these paths. ICor.12:1-11 enumerated the gifts and this is the order in which they are listed in the scriptures. The Word of Wisdom and the Word of Knowledge, (v.8) faith and the gifts of healings, (v.9) the Working of Miracles, Prophecy, Discerning of spirits, Divers

Kinds of Tongues and the Interpretation of Tongues. (v.10) We need power to do, share or say revealed truth.

So these gifts of people and gifts of the Spirit are all in the Church, latent and resident in the individual members of the local Church. We have got to stir them up by our lives, words, actions, services, kindness, mercy, compassion, encouragements, tolerance, boldness, positive aggressiveness and much more.

The Church of Jesus Christ should be the richest by divine estimation and plans, but she is not. The Roman Catholic and Mormon Organizations are the richest in our world. They are into land acquisitions, buildings, trades, business, engineering and others wealth-creating ventures around the world. What has money got to do with Ministry Gifts and the Gifts of the Holy Spirit? Every thing! God owns the earth including all who live in it, whether poor or rich and that includes you and me.

If you cannot give God your money, then it has become your god. It does not matter how much you say you love God and are willing to give your life for His cause. If you do not see any wisdom in God asking you to give to Him, then you are serving it. The writer recommends a book for you to read. It's called "Giving And Receiving" and by the same of author.

There are lawyers, engineers, doctors, nurses, bricklayers, business men and women, mothers, fathers, uncles, aunties, nephews, cousins, grand fathers and mothers, boys and girls, young men and women, old and young alike who are giving to God and the saints. Whether one has a job or not, if you are self-employed or you are an employee, you will always have money. It is either given to you, received for your work, it's your legacy, it's an allowance, it's given to you by your spouse, it's the house money in your care and however it comes. Money is not going anywhere and you will always have it. You ought to give to God out of your earnings and the remaining is for you to spend as He directs you. God gave you your life and endows you with wisdom, strength, knowledge and power to make wealth. (Deut.8:17-20)

By divine estimation, the Church of Jesus Christ ought to be the richest Body in the world if everyone who believes in Him gives. If we have a hundred member congregation and everyone of them gives to God, there will be more than enough to go round and these Ministry Gifts of men and women will be compensated for adequately, including their husbands, wives and children. We will send out evangelists, prophets, teachers, pastors and apostles, and when they come back to the body, they will recount their exploits, be ministered to, be encouraged, uplifted, charged and received ministry while the body blesses them beyond their expectation before they are sent out again.

They have come home to rest and there is no pressure on these men and women of God. This will be the end of strife, debate, dissention, pride and a do-it-your guys. There is no strife in God at all. Is there a Church that knows these things and practices them? We have become winter Christians and the Churches are empty and suffer during summer time in our congregations.

Jesus Christ is the greatest human being ever lived and He is still living even now, but outside our world. He is the richest amongst men and He owns the cattle on a thousand hills. (Psm.50:10) He is richer than all the nations of the world combined, and the earth and all of its fullness are all His. He is the One who gives men and women the power to make wealth. Then how come that the Organism, called the Church, that He has come to build is experiencing money problems? Everyone but the Church has money to finance a project that he or she wants to pursue and yet He said "the silver and gold are His." (Hag.2:8) We have a problem here because we don't have the silver and gold to do what He has asked us to do.

The Word gives us to understand that "the love of money is

the root of all evil." (1Tim.6:10) Therein lies the problem and it is in the love of money that links us to the evil. The devil is behind the evil and out of the evil comes all the misconceptions that God is not all that we need. If we think that having money is the answer to our problems, then we have got it all wrong and backwards. The love of evil leads to selfishness, cockiness, arrogance, pride and all sorts of things. I am the owner of my wealth. I worked for it. I sweated for it and it was my strength, stamina and wisdom that produced the wealth. Such reasoning forgets God and crowns himself as his own god, because behind the evil is the devil.

Humility is the answer to the love of money. Our humility under God is one of the keys to having God's abundance. We must walk under this great canopy of God and maintain this position with our heads up high. The Word says, "God resists the proud and gives grace to the humble. Humble yourself therefore under the mighty hand of God…" (1Pet.5:5-6) Humility is under God and pride is under the devil. The fact that you have placed yourself under God shows that you are not in control of your life. Someone else is controlling it and that person is not you.

That is the beginning of humility and a person who is so inclined will go a long way with God and be greatly blessed. We are not talking about humility that makes everyone to walk all over you, but the one that makes God stands up in you so that you can declare who you are in God, and what He is to you and your world. When this type of connection is formed with your Creator, then what you own is no longer yours, but God's. This is the beginning of the wealth of the saints that opens the door to the Ministries Gifts of Lord and the Gifts of the Holy Spirit.

The saints will have an awesome task with the Lord their God. They will bring the abundance of their wealth into God's family, and there shall be plenty of money for the ministry, the ministers and all who serve in the Kingdom of our Lord and Savior Jesus Christ. So do you see how the Five Fold Ministries of the Lord with the Gifts of the Spirit work in conjunction with humble spirit and the agape love of God?

God has ways and plans of doing things, and the ingathering of the human race will not be outside His plans. The system has not changed, and as it was in the beginning, even so shall it be, both now, till the close of the age. It is always God, the Father, then the Son, Jesus Christ and His Spirit, working in and through the redeemed. It has been the Word of God, then the Ministry Gift of people by Christ, and the Gifts of His Spirit. This has always been the plan, and it has not changed since the creation of the World.

In the Old Testament and all of its formative plans through the thousands of years it operated, God has always played it by the book and His rules. God's Word, His choice of men and women, and the Spirit Gifts in those people whom He has chosen, got the job done. When God sent His Son, Jesus Christ into the World, He followed the same pattern according to the plan. It was God's Word, His Gift of a person in Jesus Christ, and His Spirit filled Him with the gifts of God to get the job done. It will not be different in our days and era.

In these last days that began at the first advent of the Lord to this present era, man has to find out the ancient plan and address himself to it. The plan is God's Word, Christ Ministry Gifts of people, and His Spirit's endowment upon men and women to get the job done. Christ has to follow the pattern and make sure the disciples understood it. It is the Word of God and not man's word, the Gift of people chosen of the Lord Jesus Christ, and His Spirit's Gifts upon these men and women chosen of God.

Today, we have done it in our own ways and have discarded the original plan of God that has always been effective and brought results. We have poured thousands and millions of dollars into our own human efforts to do the works of God, and we have received little results with our human efforts. The Church must return to the original plan, and seeks the Lord God for His Ways and Thoughts in this matter.

Man cannot do divine works by using natural tools. It will not work for us, even though we pour our hearts, money and energy into it. A natural man cannot do a spiritual work using his natural human means. It will take the redeemed man, filled with the Spirit of God and His tools to get the job done. Human beings are so daft and clueless when it comes to how deep the heart of man is in wickedness. Man cannot see what he is doing wrong, because the enemy is involved in it. The mind of man has been blinded by the enemy, and that puts him in a state of spiritual ignorance. The Word says, "The natural man cannot receive the things of the Spirit of God, because they are spiritually discerned."

If we are going to effect a change and affect this world by bringing in the harvest of the souls of men and women in our generation today, we must go back to The Plan of God and retrace our steps to do the Works of God. We must use divine tools, deposited in man and controlled by the Spirit of God to close up the account of the children of men. So, it brings us to the topics we are facing in this message and they are God's Word, Jesus Christ Ministry Gifts of People, and then His Spirit and His Gifts through men and women of God. This is how we are going to get the job done and bring about the Community's Transformation in our villages, towns, cities, nations and the world. If we insist that we will do it with our own tools and by our ways, we shall fall on our faces, and eat the sand under our feet.

God is the operator of all the systems of the world, Jesus Christ is the administrator of all the Ministries Gifts of people and His Spirit is the Enforcer and He brings His gifts to man. The manifestations of the Gifts of His Spirit are the sole prerogative of the Father, and He works in ways that mankind cannot understand.

The Pentecostals, the Methodists, the Baptists, the Presbyterians, the Roman Catholics, the Evangelicals, Mormons, Jehovah Witnesses, Lutherans, Mennonites, the Anglicans, the Reforms, Denominational Churches and all the Churches in the world today will succeed and archive greater things for God, if they will do it God's Ways and use God's tools and gifts. Instead, man's enemy has infiltrated their ranks and files, and has sown seeds of misunderstanding, strife and division amongst them. They cannot see that they are ineffective and they are not doing God a service at all. We must all return to the plan of God, and submit ourselves to it, regardless of our denominational slant or bias.

THE ANCIENT PATTERN

The God-head rules the world of spirits, angels, cherubim, seraphim, man and beasts. The Father God is the Almighty Creator of all things and His Son, Jesus Christ and His Spirit are with Him in all His creative ways. The Father is not the Son and the Son is not His Spirit, but they shared the Spirit. They work together in perfect harmony and they are flawless in Beauty and Elegance.

There is no strife, division, schism and pride in them as it is seen amongst humanity. God, the Father is looking for this type of relationship among His children who are the descendants of Adam. Can humanity live under God and exhibit a flawless relationship amongst themselves and one another? That is why God is building a family or race of people with this type of identity and uniqueness. God always has reasons and plans for His actions, and He always thinks things through before He executes them. He cannot be caught with an oops, "I made a blunder and a booboo!" That is not God that we serve.

The Angels: God's Word has always been precious and He has elevated and magnified His Word above His Name.

(Psm.138:2c) Angels know one thing and this is obedience to the Lord God who has created them. Although they have a will and can choose to exercise it, they are very loyal to God. Case in point is Lucifer, who exercised his will against the will of God, and he carried out the first rebellion ever known in history. He was instrumental in the fall of man and plunged humanity into a pit of darkness that necessitates the coming of a Saviour. They receive the Word from God and deliver the message as it is given to them. They do not ask questions and why they have to go to some place. This is what God wants to do in the Church towards reclaiming the human race back to Himself.

Adam: He was created by God and given the breath of life in the first advent of His Spirit. He was given knowledge, wisdom, understanding, power and whatever it takes to be God's deputy on earth through the Spirit. He named all the animals and gave them the names that they are called even today. As God spoke to him, he carried out the divine instructions to the letter and never deviated from it. He was an example of a perfect man obeying His Creator, until sin came into the Garden, by the way of Lucifer and he fell. (Gen.2:7 and 19-20) Obedience to God was also his meat and drink, and he would have lived forever, but something happened to him. He saw God face to face, and He always visited with him in the cool of the day, and there was nothing they could not talk about. (Gen.3:8)

O.T. Prophets: God continued to speak to the prophets His Word and they delivered it promptly. There were no "ifs and buts" about the message they received from the Lord, and as they received it, they delivered the same to the people He has instructed them to give the message to. As long as they obeyed God, the sky is the limit to how far they could go in Him. God used them in super human fits and did all kinds of miracles through them. They raised the dead, cleansed lepers, fed through divine hands, dried up seas and rivers and others mind-blowing miracles were done by them. One example was that of Isaiah who made a dough of figs to heal a dying king. (Isa.38:1-22)

The God-Man: Jesus Christ: Jesus Christ was before Abraham and has always existed with God. (Jn.1:1-2 and 8:58) He was living in heaven with God. His Father sent Him to this earth to bring His children back home through the shedding of His blood and the death of His life. First we have the Word of God, secondly, we have God's choice of Man in the Person of the Lord Jesus Christ, and thirdly, His Spirit came upon Him and fill Him to overflow. He was in Him and His nine Gifts were present.

Through the Spirit of God, He performed wonders and all kinds of miracles. The dead were raised, lepers cleansed, crippled healed, thousands fed, water changed into wine, and demons were cast out of people. If the miracles performed by the Spirit through Him were to be written, the whole world would not contain it were it a book. He knows nothing, but obedience to the Word of God and total submission to His Spirit.

The Gospel exploded through Him and for three and half years of ministry, the whole world knew that He was here. After His death, He chose twelve disciples to carry on where He has stopped, and designated them as His Apostles. Lest they forgot, He told them that God's work must be done in God's ways, using God's tools and Gifts. He told them to wait for the endowment of His Spirit from on High as His Father has promised Him. (Lk.24:49, Jn.14:15-20, 16:7-14)

N.T. The Apostles/Prophets: Jesus Christ said, "As the Father has sent Me, even so send I you." (Jn.20:21) He had many disciples, but He chose twelve men to be His Apostles, and they were to do the work the way He did it. If they tried to do it in their own ways, they would fail woefully. The work must be done through men and women chosen of God and endued with the Spirit of God. The Apostles waited according to the promise of God in Acts.2:1-11, God came through with His promise, and they were commissioned from on high to do God's works in God's ways by the tools God supplied. Peter, James, John, Thomas and the untimely Paul, all received the Spirit and did what Jesus Christ did when He was in our world.

They raised the dead, cleansed lepers, made the crippled whole, opened the eyes of the blind, received miraculous provision of God, and went through their world with the Gospel of Christ. They did what they were told by the Spirit of God, and the book of the Bible in their honor that was called the Acts of the Apostles was not really their acts, but the acts of the Spirit of God through them. So the pattern was also followed and they duplicated the life of Jesus Christ.

The Church Today: The Apostles passed the torch of Christ that was given to them by God, the Father to the Church today. We have proliferations of Churches in our world, and they all have pastors, teachers, prophets, evangelists and apostles who are following their denominational agenda and calling. There are few ministers who stick to the divine agenda and adhere to the ancient plan of the Living God. If we will succeed, we have to do it the way that the angels, Adam, the prophets, the Lord Jesus Christ and the Apostles of the Lord did it.

The Word says, "Obedience is better than sacrifice and to hearken than the fatlings of rams." They had the Word of the Lord, they were chosen of Christ as His gifts of people to His Body, and they obey the Spirit of God as He gave them His manifestations to bring wholeness, healing and sanity to our world, gathering the souls of humanity to God for a harvest of all ages. This is how the harvest of the souls of the world will be gathered to God, our Father. It is going to be His way or else we can get out of the path, street, way or line for those who will receive the mandate of heaven and get the job done.

We must forget our denominations, churches, religion, tribes, societal nom, secrecy to which we have sworn, pride, the way we have been doing it and stick to the plan of God. In it hinges, the power, wisdom, understanding, strength, knowledge, happiness, joy, love, inspiration, favor and all that we need to get the job done.

COMMUNITY TRANSFORMATION

In today's Christendom, we have not come close to the dedication, devotion and zeal of the first century saints. We fall short of their prayer life, commitment, the life of fasting and spiritual fervency. If we must have Community Transformation, we need to do better than what we have today. Can we compare ourselves with the O.T saints like Isaiah, Jeremiah, Ezekiel and Daniel? We are dwarfed by their sincerity and spirituality. If God is going to transform our city and change the community, we have got to show some dedication and devotion to the ways and the will of God in the following areas. Charity must begin at home with our wives and husbands, our money and work ethics, our business and how we trade, our dedication and commitment to God beyond what we have now. It will take all we have by way of surrendering our body, soul and spirit to the living God.

We need to be rising up early in the morning like Jesus Christ did before His Father and spent some time pouring His heart out before Him and listening to His voice. Prayer is our admission that He has the answers to the problems of this world, and He is willing and ready to reveal and show us the way. We do not have what it takes to confound the world's wisdom. (1Cor.1:17-31)

We have to be in line with the will of God and make sure that when we make a vow, that we meet the conditions of the vows we made before our God. We have to take seriously our giving to God, who willingly gave us all that we have. It is important that we give to God as He commands us to.

The Lord Jesus Christ said of the Holy Communion that we

should do this in remembrance of Him. We do it solemnly and very often in our homes and Churches. It is a time of healing and comfort in the Lord. It gives us the assurance and the certainty that God owns the day and Christ wants us to remember what He did for us when He came into this world. It is the writer's opinion that in every home of the believers, communion should be taken every day in keeping with the expression of the Lord Jesus Christ.

Our devotion and commitment to God should be such that we cannot have enough of Him, and as such, we go on a periodic days or weeks of prayer and fasting away from our busy home and regular schedules. We take time out of our business to have a spiritual holiday with God alone in prayer, fasting and consecration to Him for His direction for our lives, and the things we so more desire for His glory and honor.

As the children of God, we have to live a life of sharing and giving of the Gospel, our money, time, love and all that is within our reach. This is what it will take to have a personal, individual, city and community transformation. If it does not come from our homes and hearts, we cannot take it to the community in a way that it will affect our city and transforms the one and half million souls that live in Winnipeg.

We spend thousands and millions of dollars in building Bible Colleges and Seminaries, and send our sons and daughters to them. Men and women of God are pouring their hearts out to these students, and we turn out hundreds and thousands of Bible College and Seminary students every year. Has it ever occurred to us that we are teaching them half-truths? We minor on our majors and major on our minors. We have not truly and honestly presented the Plan of God to the students who will later on become the pastors, prophets, evangelists, apostles and teachers of tomorrow.

We are teaching them to know our denominational bias and

slant, and not the Plan of God. An average Bible College or Seminary student does not know the God and Father of our Lord Jesus Christ by experience. He or she has not met Him in the privacy of their prayers in order for the Lord to speak to him as to what He wants done in his life.

Revelation is not encouraged and both scientific and empirical methods of finding God through human efforts are greatly coveted. We have not emphasized the God who gives His Word, then the Gifts of People whom He has chosen to do His work and finally, His Spirit and gifts upon these individuals that Jesus Christ has called to be with Him, before they can go out to be with people. (Mk.3:14) We know a lot of man's systems, but nothing of God. May be we are afraid of work and are lazy to seek the Lord. It could be that we are afraid that the Lord might just show up if we seek Him diligently, and change the course of our lives. May be we like to be in control, and if we differ to the Lord, He might just take away our control, and there will nothing for us to do. Whatever the reasons, we are not succeeding in this venture and we need to find a different way of doing evangelism. Man's ways have failed woefully.

What about our world and its denominational walls that we have built to keep God in His Church. Although, the Church is not an organization, but an Organism, a living, breathing, walking and talking specimen, created in the image of God and after His likeness. We have erected our denominational structures and limited the Holy One to what we can see, feel, taste, handle, smell, hear and touch. We have thrown away the concept of a God who speaks and reveals Himself as to what He wants done in this world of His. Someone says. "Denomination is an abomination unto God." How true is this statement? It creates the polarization of Churches and the people of God. It casts each one of us into different camps and having understanding which are opposite of the basic truths and knowledge of the Lord.

We have set our camps and called them: Baptist, Anglican, Methodist, Presbyterian, Pentecostal, Salvation Army, Roman Catholic, Tabernacle of Lord, Orthodox Church, United Church and many more that the writer cannot remember. May the Lord have mercy on us and forgive our pride and ignorance of His ways and methods. There is no division in God and therefore all His children are not divided, even though they are uniquely different. God is different, yet He and His Son are not divided, and their differences do not affect their functions and personalities. Humanity likes to take ownership of things, but not in God. We cannot take ownership of the things pertaining to God and His Spirit. Taking ownership in matters relating to God and His Spirit is an abomination to the Lord of heaven. Denomination prevents us from seeing the Plan of God, and it focuses on our individual and collective efforts within the confines of the sect to pursue our own goals, seeking ways of doing the Works of God, instead of asking Him directly regarding His plans for our lives.

We must stick to His Plan of harvesting souls into the Kingdom and throw overboard our own plans for the wisdom and revelation of God to get the job done. The plan has not changed and it is still the Word of God, the Ministry Gifts of people by the Lord Jesus Christ, His Spirit and manifestations to the men and women of God. This was how the Angels did it. Adam followed in their steps and did it before the evil one deceived him. The OT saints of Prophets, teachers and scribes also followed the plan of God.

Lord Jesus Christ, the last Adam did it just like the prophets of old. The apostles followed the steps of the Lord and extended the Ministry of Jesus Christ with the same results. Today, we cannot do it differently and we must follow the Apostles of the Lord, if we want the same results. If we must gather the souls of humanity for God, then, we must use God's tools and follow His ways. (Isa.55:6-12)

Why are we surprised if God does something that does not fit our status quo? Why do we think God could do miracles in the days of Isaiah, Jeremiah, Paul, Peter, John and Jesus Christ, but cannot do it in our days? Is God only the God of yesterday and not the God of today? Have we limited the Holy One of Israel as to what He can and cannot do? Can God open the prison doors like He did for Peter? Can some of the children of God still walk on water as He did in the days of Christ, if there is need for it? The answer to all these questions and more is yes, yes and yes. God can do any and every thing that will bring glory to His name and bring His children home to Him.

He has raised the dead in the continent of Africa, Asia, North and South America, Europe and other places in our century. If He can raise the dead, then all other miracles are a piece of cake for Him to perform. There are mind bugling and blowing testimonies all over the world, and even a tenth of the wonders of God has not been told. What will the writer tell you about different Chinese, Japanese, Nigerians, Koreans saints and other nations that have been beaten with rods and sledge hammers, put into boiling oil, locked up in boxes of nails, cast into icy waters for days and are still living to tell of the wonders of God and of His Christ.

We have to ask Him to enlarge our capacity to know Him and make Him known in all of His wonders, compassion, mercy, favor, might, wisdom, knowledge, purity, righteousness and grace. If we trust in Him, and yet, He does not deliver us, it is a promotion to glory. He is too great and gigantic for human mind to comprehend. It is like a drop of water surveying the depth of all the bodies of water put together in this world and beyond. It cannot and it must not try. The human race combined is like a drop of water and God is like the body of all waters put together in the world. It will blow your mind trying to understand the enormity and the power of our God.

Chapter Sixteen

GOD'S SPIRIT WORKING WITH HIS CHURCH

The book of Acts was given to us to show what God will do through those who will trust in His Spirit to lead, guide and control them. It was really the acts of God, through His Spirit by men and women who were collectively called the Church or the people of God.

Jesus Christ had given commandments to the Apostles, a small group of men called the Church, and this was where Christ began to build His Church. (Acts.1:2) God's Spirit was promised to the disciples. He would come upon them to empower them in witnessing to the ministry, passion, death, resurrection and the ascension of Christ. Right from the page of the Acts of the Apostles, the Church was expanding, growing and increasing by the power of the Spirit of God. Peter and John made the lame man to walk, not by their own power, but the Spirit's. (Acts.3)

In punitive miracles, the Apostles, and the Spirit confirmed their words. Ananias and Sapphira, his wife, died suddenly. (Acts.5) Saul of Tarsus struck with blindness on the road to Damascus. (Acts.9) Herod died. He was eaten by worms through the hands of the angel of God. (Acts.12) He died because he was playing God as a man. Elymas, the false prophet was blinded, because he was opposing the word of the Lord. (Acts.13)

Just as in the Gospel of Luke, the Spirit of God inspired, performed and guided all the miracles in Acts. The rightful name of the Book should be called, "The Acts of the Spirit of God".

- Jesus instructs the apostles "through the Holy Spirit". (1:2)
- The first disciples are "baptized with the Spirit" at Pentecost. (1:5, 8; 2:1-4; 11:15-16)
- The apostles are "full of" or "filled with" the Holy Spirit, when they preach. (1:8; 2:4; 4:8, 31; 11:24; 13:9, 52)
- Similarly, the Holy Spirit spoke through king David and the prophets in ancient Israel. (1:16; 4:25; 28:25)
- God "will pour out" his Spirit on all people and all nations in the last days. (2:17-18, 33; 10:45)
- Believers, including Gentiles, receive the Holy Spirit when they repented and are baptized. (2:38; 15:8; 19:5-6)
- Sometimes the reception of the Holy Spirit even precedes baptism. (10:44-48)
- Some people "test" or "lie to" or "oppose" the Holy Spirit, with dire consequences. (5:1-11; 7:51)
- Deacons and other ministers must also be "full of the Spirit" (6:1-6), especially when they prophesy. (6:10; 7:55-59; 11:28; 21:4)
- The Spirit is conferred through the "laying on of hands". (8:17-19; 9:17; 19:6)
- The Spirit "speaks to" the apostles and prophets. (8:29; 10:19; 11:12; 13:1-4; 21:11)
- The Spirit leads and guides the decisions and actions of the Christian leaders. (15:28; 16:6-7; 19:21; 20:22-23)

The Spirit of God was moving through the Church of Jesus Christ, and by the hands of the Apostles, He did many signs and wonders. The Church contained the Apostles, and not the Apostles the Church. See the miracles wrought through the Apostles by the Spirit of God.

THE CHURCH

BACK FROM THE DEAD ACTS.

1. Peter raises Tabitha — 9:36-46
2. Paul raises the young man Eutychus — 20:9-12

CURES AND EXORCISMS

1. Peter heals the lame man at the Temple gate — 3:1-16
2. Ananias cures Saul of his blindness — 9:17-18
3. Peter heals the paralytic Aeneas — 9:33-35
4. Paul cures the lame man of Lystra — 14:7-9
5. Paul stoned and miraculously healed at Lystra — 14:19
6. Paul exorcises girl possessed of divining spirit — 16:16-18
7. Paul heals Publius' father of dysentery — 28:7-8

PUNITIVE MIRACLES

1. Ananias and Sapphira struck dead at Peter's feet — 5:5-11
2. Saul struck blind on the road to Damascus — 9:8-9
3. Herod suddenly slain by an angel — 12:23
4. Paul temporarily blinds the sorcerer, Elymas — 13:9-12

COSMIC MIRACLES

1. Violent wind at the Pinnacle in Jerusalem — 2:2-6
2. Shaking of the assembly building in Jerusalem — 4:31
3. Prison doors open for the Apostles — 5:17-25
4. Philip snatched by the Spirit of the Lord — 8:39
5. Peter liberated from prison by an angel — 12:5-11
6. Chains fall from Paul and Silas — 16:25-30
7. Paul shakes off viper from his arm — 28:3-6

PLURAL MIRACLES

Many signs and wonders done by the Apostles in Jerusalem.	2:43
Apostles perform signs and wonders among the people	5:12
Peter's shadow cures many in the streets	5, 15
Multitudes from outside Jerusalem are healed	5:16
Stephen works great signs and wonders	6:8
Philip cures crippled and possessed in Samaria	8:6-8, 13
Miracles worked by Paul and Barnabas on the missionary journey	14:3
Great signs and wonders done among the Gentiles	15:12
Miracles worked through objects touched by Paul	19:11-12
Paul heals all the sick brought to him on Malta	28:9

Chapter Seventeen

AN ALTERNATIVE WAY OF FELLOWSHIP

People have gotten so used to the way we carry out what the world called "Church" that it may seem strange to suggest that there is an alternative way the Church should function. The alternative way is actually the New Testament way. Back then believers gathered primarily in homes to make disciples, to fellowship and worship together, and to share their lives and experience Christ together. Each believer having received the Holy Spirit and being a part of the body of Christ, all came to participate and use their gifts to build each other up.

Jesus led and taught them by the Holy Spirit, which allowed Him to live in and function through each believer. There were no special church buildings, no special day to meet, nor any paid leaders with special titles - only ministry functions in the body of Christ. More matured believers helped to oversee the Churches, but no believer had authority over any other believer, for they were all brothers and sisters in God's family.

Believers loved one another, gathered and ate together, and shared what they had with one another as a family. They also shared their hearts and struggles with one another, so that they could pray for one another to receive encouragement, practical help, freedom and healing by the power and authority of Jesus' name. This was the simple New Testament way of life and support system for the family of God (His Church) through meeting in homes.

Unfortunately after the original apostles of Jesus died, the mainstream Church began to stray from this simple New Testament model. Overseers took on positions of authority over other believers as Apostles, Prophets, Pastors, arch Bishops, Bishops and began to control and direct the Church where they wanted her to go. The Church leaders (Popes, Bishops, Priests, Pastors) also took control of the meetings and began including their own ideas and traditions into their teaching.

They disallowed believers to fully participate and added a formal service where believers had to sit and learn what the leaders taught them. Special church buildings (Basilicas) were made for believers to meet in and a special day was given for believers to meet. (Sundays) A religious tax (Tithing) was also charged to maintain the buildings and support those running the organization.

The leaders prohibited believers from meeting in their own homes or on their own. Instead of following the lead of Jesus Christ and obeying him as the head, believers were told to follow and obey the leaders. The Church has remained much the same for the past 1700 years, and this Church model is accepted by most believers as the way it is meant to be. Unfortunately this is not what Jesus and his apostles taught in the New Testament, which has stopped Jesus from functioning as the leader and head of His Church.

Today more and more believers around the world are asking the Church to return to the New Testament model, where resources can be shared with those who truly need it, and Christ can once again be the head of His Church and function through His Church body as he intended.

Today, we have super pastors, ministers, administrators, builders of churches, ache-apostles, bishops, deacons, rich men and women who have founded the churches and called them as their own.

Cathedrals, mega structures, temples, buildings and such like which have multiple usages. Do not only house people for the worship of God, but also Church related businesses. These have formed the most viable businesses today among the God fearing individuals. Men and women owning planes, yachts, fabulous houses, acres of land by the seas and lakes, statesmen and women who have risen to the top 3% of the wealth of our nations.

Christian ministers are no longer called by the ways that the Spirit of God uses them, but by the size of their wallets. The Church is becoming worldly and the world is becoming churchy, and no one can tell who is who in Christendom.

Chapter Eighteen

BASIC PRINCIPLES OF THE NEW TESTAMENT CHURCH

RON FISCHER
By Permission

The basis for truth and practices were the teachings of Jesus of Nazareth, and the guidelines of the original apostles as recorded in the New Testament.

The Church was not a building, nor a place, but instead, the Church is people who believed in Jesus as the Christ, and followed Him as their Leader. They were born again in their spirit from above and had received the Holy Spirit, who lived in them. Jesus led them and taught them by the Holy Spirit.

Believers met in homes many days of the week (no special day) as a family, to eat together, learn together, worship together, and experience Jesus in their midst. They helped out one another, and prayed for one another and their community. They all participated in the meetings.

Each believer had ministry and spiritual gifts from the Holy Spirit to be used, to build up one another, minister healing and freedom, and share the good news to the world. They had functions of service - not special titles or positions of authority. No believer had authority over any other believer.

Some believers were trained and sent out as apostles to share the gospel in the market place, gather new Churches with those that believed, then laid a foundation on the teachings of Christ, and guidelines of the original apostles as recorded in the New Testament.

Believers did not tithe, but instead gave freely and generously to those who were in need, (the elderly, the disabled, and poor believers who had no family to help support them) and towards preaching the good news. (Traveling workers)

Some mature believers (elders) functioned as overseers, shepherds to help care for, protect, mentor, and guide the Church. They did not have authority over the Church being among the people of God, with Jesus as the leader. Believers showed appreciation to them, listened to their council, yet obedience was first given to Jesus, who was the Great Overseer.

Some mature believers functioned as social workers, deacons, deaconesses to help care for the practical needs of believers: the elderly, the disabled, poor believers who had no family to help support them.

All believers worked to support themselves and their families (including overseers and deacons) in order to be able to give to those who are truly in need. When travelling on mission trips, believers stayed with other believers, who took care of their needs, and they may have received an occasional monetary gift from the Churches they visited and ministered to. However, when they stayed in one place for a time, they would work to support themselves, so that they were not a financial burden to the Church body.

Believers loved the Lord with all their heart, soul, mind and strength, and they loved one another as a family. Believers made community decisions by seeking God's will together, and dealt with problems as a group together, including closing the doors to people that were harming the Church. (False teachers leading people astray, people who wanted to control others, and those who were living in sin and would not repent).

CHURCHES FILLING THE CITY
(1,000,000 HOUSE CHURCHES)

The Goal: Millions of millions of Home Churches in the city from the North, South, East and West. She will occupy a notable place of honor before God, and a catalyst to the city, province and Nation in terms of its population and the way of life.

Sizable Goal: Reality: We will start with 50, 100, 150, 200 and beyond, of House Churches, and she will grow in strength, wisdom, power and might of the Lord.

Shepherd: God is the Shepherd of His flock and Jesus Christ is watching over all by the spirit of God. Apostles, prophets, evangelists, pastors and teachers will flow according to the will of God.

Priesthood: Everyone who has met Jesus Christ, and in love with Him, and has come under His Lordship, having Him as the Lord, Redeemer and Savior of their lives, will come forward to honor His name.

Groups of 2-10: The city will have as its goal 2-10 or 10-15 meeting in houses just like the NT Church. The body will have the opportunity to excel in love, ministry, worship, spontaneity, prophecy, gifts of the spirit and much more.

No Building: There will be no building to maintain, no over head cost, no hydro bills, heating bills, repairs, paying salaries to 8-10 people from the senior pastor to the custodian.

Money Matter: The Church will have money to do what she has always wanted to do, and be able to reach out to the poor, the needy, the orphans, widows, fatherless, and take care of her own responsibilities.

Interactions: The Church will meet not just one or two times a week, but often in person, through telephone, through email, through letter writing, visits, in coffee shops and house meetings.

God's Gifts: This will create rumblings in the spiritual and physical worlds, and the community, society and people will take notice of the Lord Christ and His Father, the Creator of all things. City Church will be one and Christ will be over all His saints.

Chapter Nineteen

GOD AND BUILDING

(ACTS.7:49)

God is a relational Being and in the beginning, He was fellowshipping and communicating with the first pair of humanity, according to Gen.3:8. He came to Adam and Eve in the cool of the day, until sin marred the relationship, and humanity was separated from His Maker. (Gen.2:16-17; 3:1-7) God had intended to continue in this fellowship with mankind in Adam, but it was cut short by the pair, and man entered into an era of darkness in which he was fending for himself, removed from the Spirit of God that made him.

Adam had three sons, Cain, Abel and Seth, but the first two died. The first killed the second, and he was banished from the presence of the Lord forever, being the first to shed human blood in death on the earth. (Gen.4:10-15) But in the days of the third, who was Seth, and in the birth of his first son, called Enosh, men began to call upon the Name of the Lord. Men were having fellowship and relationship with God again. (Gen.4:25-5:32) This relationship continued until a man was taken up into heaven in a human form without dying. The name of this man was Enoch and the Lord enjoyed the fellowship so much that they had to carry on the conversation elsewhere or another venue. (Gen.5:24)

In Gen.6, mankind began to multiply on earth, and their sins grew to an alarming proportion. God then decided that He would obliterate mankind from the surface of the earth, because his heart was continuously evil. (Gen.6:5-8) But Noah found favor in the sight of the Lord, and He preserved him, his wife, his three sons and their wives totaling eight in numbers.

Noah got drunk with wine, and his son, Ham, saw his nakedness. (Gen.9:20-29) Several hundreds of years passed and God called Abraham, the great, great grandson of Seth, but before then, the whole earth was of one language. They began to build a tower whose top would reach into heaven where God dwelt. They would have succeeded, had not God confused their language. (Gen.11)

God vowed that He would make a name for Abraham. Kings and princes would come out of his loins. What man was going to do by his own strength, He would do through Abraham, and his off-springs. (Gen.12-50) Genesis chapters 12-50 are the stories of Abraham descendants.

We have Isaac, the son of Abraham, Jacob, the son of Isaac and then Moses, the son of Amram and Jochebed. (Exo.2:1-7; 6:20 and Num.26:59-60) These were the stories of Israel's exodus that Moses led from Egypt to the Promised Land. The Hebrews were led by God through the hand of Moses, from the land of tyranny, into the Promised Land, He promised them.

God said that His presence would be and walk amongst His people, but not in a mega structure, instead in a shifting tent. God told Moses to build the Tabernacle in exact specifications like the real thing he saw in heaven. God moved with His people and was in their midst in a movable tent called Tabernacle. The Temple of Solomon was a re-enactment of the Tabernacle in the wilderness.

In 1Sam.7:1-29, when the Lord had given rest to David from all his enemies around, he purposed in his heart to build a resting place for the Ark of the Covenant which symbolized the presence of God. Primarily David had a genuine desire to build something more fitting for the King of kings, who is more to him and his throne. Secondly the king was feeling uncomfortable, because God was dwelling in a tent, while he, a mere man, was living in a palace. (1Chro.28:2; 2Sam.7:5; 1Chro.17:4 and 28:3)

The first Temple was built by king Solomon, and it was destroyed by the Babylonians in 587 BC. The second Temple was built by Zerubbabel, and it was destroyed in A.D. 70, under Herod, the great, by the Romans, under Emperor Titus. When Christ was dying on the cross, the presence of God left the Temple, signifying that He was not please with the Old Order of things. Since then, He wants to dwell in the human hearts, a temple, not built with the hands of man with mortals, bricks, nails, wood, cement and iron. (Matt.27:51-54, Mk.15:37-38 and Lk.23:44-47)

Looking at the Church of Jesus Christ today, we are far removed from the heart of God, and we have erected for ourselves monuments, structures, cathedrals and mega buildings, we have designated as the house of God. The word of God echo through the ages, and He wanted humanity to know that: "Heaven is My throne and the earth is My footstool: what house will you build for Me? What is the place of My rest?" says the Lord. My hands have made all things, including the earth and the humans on it.

They took the Lord's Supper as a full meal. (1Cor.11:21-34) Their Church gatherings were open and participatory. (1Cor.14:26; Heb.10:24-25) Spiritual gifts were by the Spirit through each member. (1Cor.12-14) They genuinely saw themselves as family and acted accordingly. (Gal.6:10; 1Tim.5:1-2; Rom.12:5, 13; Eph.4:15; 1Cor.12:25-26, 2Cor.8:12-15) They had a plurality of elders to oversee the community. (Acts.20:17, 28-29; 1Tim.1:5-7)

They were established and aided by itinerant apostolic workers. (Acts.13-21. All the apostolic letters) They were fully united and did not denominate themselves into separate organizations in the same city. (Acts.8:1, 13:1, 18:22; Rom.16:1; 1Thes.1:1) They did not use honorific titles. (Matt.23:8-12) They did not organize themselves hierarchically. (Matt.20:25-28; Lk.22:25-26) We imported our programs and order of services from the pagan world.

We go to a Church building every Sunday morning and go through the motions without considering why we do what we do. We repeat the squabbles, the fights, the commotions, misunderstanding and the struggles without ever asking ourselves why do we do these things? We have been influenced far more by post-biblical historical events than New Testaments principles. We know that early Church met in homes for their regular Church meetings. (Acts.20:20; Rom.16:3, 5; 1Cor.16:19)

Chapter Twenty

HOUSE CHURCH FELLOWSHIPS

LEADERSHIP

The word "Church" means "assembly or gathering". The first Church met in the homes of Christians to celebrate Jesus Christ, and the forms this celebration took vary, but she was involved in praying, singing of hymns, spiritual songs, reading of Scriptures, sharing meals together, healing, words of exaltation, encouragement, the gifts of the Spirit, and many other stuffs orchestrated by the Spirit of God. The glory, honor and the Lordship of Jesus Christ were the central core of this community.

There were leaders of these House Churches, and their names were mentioned in the Scriptures as well as the city where they were. Although little is known of them, they were remembered as early followers of Christ, who opened their homes for Christian fellowships or who led local groups of Christians in House Churches.

Training, education and mentorship are very important for an individual to take on the role of being a facilitator, moderator, coordinator or House Church Leader, but it does not mean a paper qualification. Twelve men went to Christ's School, and it did not involve paper qualification. These 12 men were with the

Lord for three and half years. They were under authority before they could be in authority.

LEADER	CITY	SCRIPTURE
Phoebe	Cenchreas	Rom.16:1-2
Gaius	Corinth	Rom.16:23, 1Cor.1:14 Cor.16:19
Philemon	Colossae	Phile.1:2
Nympha	Laodicea	Col.4:15
Phillip Barnabas,	Caesarea	Acts.21:8
Simeon & Co	Antioch	Acts.13:1-2
Titus	Crete	Titus.1:4-6
Lydia	Thyatira	Acts.16:8
Elders	Thessalonica	Acts.14:23, Thes.1:1ff
Timothy	Ephesus	1Tim.1:3
The Jailer	Philippian / Lystra	Acts.16:25-34
John Mark's Mother	Jerusalem	Acts.12:12-17

Millions of millions Church Houses in the cities from the North, South, East and West. She will occupy a notable place of honor before God and a catalyst to the city, province and Nation in terms of its population and the way of life.

GORDON COULSON
(He's With the Lord)

Many people today are searching for more meaningful Christian fellowship. Some belong to a traditional Church, but are no longer getting their spiritual needs met. Others are new to Christianity, but are not interested in joining a traditional Church for various reasons. And some are survivors of abusive religious systems, and are reluctant to join another organization. Where can people like these turn? The answer for many has been House Church. But what is house church? Is it biblical?

WHAT IS HOUSE CHURCH?

The word Church in the New Testament is a translation of the Greek ecclesia, which means an assembly. It refers to the people of God, not to the building. A House Church is a group of people, perhaps a dozen or so, that meet together to practice simple, informal Christianity in someone's home. Together, they pray, sing, study the Scriptures, and share meals. As they get to know one other better, they may share their most intimate problems and challenges. As the group develops and grows, they may have to split into two or more House Churches, but will usually meet periodically as a larger group.

House Churches were the norm in first century Christianity. (Rom.16:3-5, Col.4:15). The professional pastor-led and board-controlled Church of today, with its Sunday morning service and rows of people in pews would appear uninviting to Jesus' early disciples. They practiced their faith in a more intimate and informal setting.

House Church should be distinguished from cell groups. Cell groups are the traditional Church's response to the need for more intimate and meaningful fellowship. The main Church organizes several cell groups that meet during the week in homes. They will then all assemble together, usually on Sunday in the larger Church building, for their traditional denominational service. Authority is still in the hands of the head pastor, who usually appoints leaders for each of the cell groups. The agenda is often defined centrally and disseminated by the cell group leaders. Although there is more intimate and informal contact between members, which is beneficial, there is usually little room for exploration of scripture according to individual conscience or for the development of individual gifts of the Spirit.

Conversely, in a House Church, the leadership is not so clearly observable. The group is autonomous—it does not report to any governing authority, except Christ, who is the head of the congregation. (Eph.5:23) All members participate, exercising their particular gifts from God for the building up of their brothers and sisters. (1Cor.12:7) The goal is to have the meetings led by Christ through God's Spirit, and not controlled by detailed human agendas. (Matt.18:20, Gal.5:19-25)

As the body has many parts, each with a God-designed purpose, so the House Church has several members, each with God-given gifts for the building up of the body. (1Cor.12:14-28) As the Holy Spirit develops gifts in individuals, they became recognize by the other members. Some will be natural organizers; some gifted teachers; some natural evangelists; others exceptionally hospitable, and so on. The key is to have faith that Jesus will lead his own Church, and be discerning of the activity of the Spirit of God. (Eph.4:7-13)

What does a House Church Meeting look like? It will depend on the backgrounds of the members, and how the group evolved. Some House Churches look very much like a formal bible study. After prayer for God's direction, a section of scripture is read and discussed by the group. A facilitator, which should be a rotating role, will coordinate the meeting. Other groups may be more free form, with a lot of singing of praises and group prayer. The discussion and study will be dynamic—dependent on the Spirit's leadings and current needs. Some House Churches are very charismatic, praying for healing and exercising prophetic gifts. (1Cor.14:1) Most House Churches set aside time for common meals and fellowship. (Acts. 2:46)

We will typically gravitate towards a House Church that is more in line with our personal background, but we should not judge those that are different. (Lk.6:37) In fact, visiting other House Churches can be educational and edifying. We learn firsthand that the body of Christ is diverse. We learn to be more tolerant of those whose backgrounds are different than ours.

GROUPS DYNAMICS

Although House Church is generally more rewarding spiritually than the traditional Church service, it is not without its challenges. This should not be a surprise considering people are involved! A cursory look at First Corinthians demonstrates that congregation life will inevitably involve conflict. Sadly, many House Churches fail, because their members are not aware of the benefits of basic conflict resolution skills, practiced with Christian love. Knowledge of the phases of group growth, and the problems encountered at each stage, can be very helpful in addressing interpersonal issues. A useful tool for understanding group dynamics is the Forming-Storming-Norming-Performing model.

A new House Church is created when a group of people commit to meeting regularly for fellowship in someone's home. This is the Forming phase. The members are on their best behavior. There is excitement in the air—something new has begun. Each member is trying to understand what their role is within the body of Christ. Disagreements are generally not aired. Things appear to be going well, but the group is interacting only superficially.

Soon questions of leadership, agenda, roles or goals will emerge. We have entered the Storming phase. Who will facilitate the meeting? Who will host it? Who will teach? What will be the subject of discussion? In which direction are we headed? Infighting may occur and alliances form. But don't be alarmed—this is natural and a sign of growth. The key is to communicate clearly and openly with each other. (Matt.5:37) A common mistake at this stage is to ignore issues for the sake of 'peace'. They will only resurface later with greater intensity. (Matt.5:23-24) Problems and issues need to be discussed openly, if the group is to grow beyond the Storming phase.

In the Norming phase, roles are finally sorted out and the group finds new energy. Members learn what to expect from each other, and each member knows where they can best contribute. Ideally, roles will be recognized as appointed by the Holy Spirit. Elders, for example, will be those who have developed, under God's direction, the scriptural qualifications. (Titus.1:5-9, 1 Tim.3:1-7) And the roles are generally not static. One person may be qualified to teach on one subject, and another person on another subject. The role of facilitating the discussion will usually rotate.

A member who has been making good spiritual progress may now be recognized by the group as capable of exercising a role they were previously unqualified for. Conversely, someone who has regressed spiritually will now be seen as unqualified for a role they previously filled. The important point is that these various scriptural roles are raised up by God's Spirit, and are recognized by the ecclesia. They are not formal offices such as the clergy occupy in a typical Church. Sorting out the roles that Jesus Christ wants in his local ecclesia brings a welcome stability and strength to the group.

If the House Church continues to progress in the Spirit of Christian love, it will eventually achieve a mature closeness. This is the Performing phase. The members will respect each other's contributions and gifts, and will recognize and appreciate the role each plays in the building up of His Church. There will be a high level of commitment and caring. Christian freedom and principled love will abound. Members will be free to form relationships with those external to the group without the group feeling threatened. Problems and issues are clearly identified and discussed. This local body of Christ will be a true reflection of the life of Jesus in an ungodly world, and a place of refuge for those seeking God. The group will increasingly look outward for opportunities to represent Jesus in the community.

However, as a car requires regular maintenance, the group must keep itself healthy and functioning. As new members join, old members leave, or the group takes on new tasks, it will tend to revert to earlier phases of development. Issues of leadership, agenda, roles or goals will again arise. We should not be discouraged when the group seems to regress, but recognize this as normal dynamics. Experience will teach us that through gentle and patient pastoring, the House Church will again rise to the level of mature closeness and harmony.

DOCTRINES/TEACHINGS

Typical House Churches are comprised of people from different traditions. This variety provides an opportunity for enhanced learning, and it is encouraged, but it also presents challenges. Some may feel very strongly about teachings that others view as optional or even unscriptural. How does a House Church deal with such potentially provocative issues?

There are usually three concerns Christians have regarding doctrine. The first is unity, the second is orthodoxy, and the third is message. Many feel that a common doctrinal system is needed to reduce disagreements. There are concerns that if safeguards are not put in place, the House Church will drift from "orthodoxy" into "heresy". Related to these two concerns are questions about the message: How can a Church evangelize, if it doesn't have a common Gospel? These are valid concerns and we will address each one in turn.

First, it should be understood that true unity occurs when Christians love one another deeply and are Christ-centered, not just by signing a common doctrinal statement. (1Cor.8:1-3, Phil.2:1-3, Eph.4:15) Jesus Christ commands us to love one another, (Jn.13:34-35, Rom.13:8) but sadly many Christians spend more energy justifying their doctrinal position or trying to convert others to it than obeying Him in this matter. Most issues of unity would disappear if Christians practiced more love in their fellowships, focused more on Jesus, and spent less time on theological debates. (2Tim.2:14)

What About Orthodoxy?
Shouldn't Christians strive for "orthodox" belief?

"Orthodoxy" and "heresy" are relative concepts, and are deeply misunderstood by most Christians. The idea that historic Christianity had a common, homogenous doctrinal position, is a myth. Scholars now understand that Christianity of the first few centuries had a rich and varied tradition. "Orthodox" came to refer to those with the most power, and "heretics" are those that resisted them. John Wycliffe, William Tyndale and John Huss were all considered heretics in their day, (the latter two were burned at the stake by the "orthodox" Church) but are now considered saints. We should reject the terms "orthodox" and "heretic" as being relative, unhelpful and misleading.

So are we then to follow post-modern relativism? Should

House Churches be a confused market place of ideas, no matter how absurd? Certainly not! We are commanded to worship in spirit and truth. (Jn.4:24) Paul warns of those who would try to suppress the truth or who would not obey the truth. (Rom.1:18, 2:8) But what exactly is this truth?

Many Christians think of "the Truth" as a doctrinal system. But note that Jesus claimed to be the way, the truth and the life. (Jn.14:6) Being "in the truth" does not mean to adhere to some theological system, but refers to being united to Christ in discipleship. It is He that reveals himself to us by the Spirit and the word of God, and through him, we come to know the Father and His purposes. (Jn.14:7-11) The center of Christianity is Christ, not a theological system purported to be based on Scripture. (Jn.5:39)

READING AND DISCUSSING SCRIPTURES

Of course Jesus and his apostles did leave us a body of teaching in the New Testament. We need to prayerfully study and discuss it, using a good Bible translation, while asking God to enlighten our minds and hearts. We should be careful not to impose our ideas on Scripture, but rather let Scriptures speak to us in its original context. Considering the writer's purpose and his reader's probable understanding is much more profitable than picking out isolated Scriptures that appear to support our personal ideas. The latter practice often leads to a misunderstanding or even a subversion of Scripture.

Another helpful principal is to divide teachings into essential and non-essential. Essential doctrine is that which is crucial for salvation as defined by Scripture. For example, the teaching that Jesus is the Christ, the Son of God, is essential and non-negotiable. (Matt.16:16, Acts.8:37) The belief that Christians are under the Law of Moses is not. (Rom.6:14, Gal.5:18)

Another good principal is "two or three witnesses." (Matt.18:16) If two or three Scriptures, taken in context, agree, and there are no clear contradictory Scriptures, we can assume the teaching is sound. If contradictions are found, however, we may have to suspend belief or reject the teaching.

Finally, it is important to see how the New Testament writers interpret the Old Testament. We need to follow the same pattern. For example, many Scriptures which originally applied to Israel are reinterpreted to apply to Christians. (see Exo.19:6 and 1Pet.2:9) The Old Testament points forward to Christ, and the New Testament proclaims he has arrived. In Jesus, all of God's purposes come to fruition, and this needs to be kept in mind, especially when reading the Old Testament.

THE GOSPEL

Essential teaching is tied to the Gospel. What do we tell others who are interested in Jesus? We should have a consistent message. If we examine the cases of conversion in the New Testament, we will glean some important information regarding essential teaching and the Gospel. To him [Jesus] all the prophets bear witness that in everyone, putting faith in him gets forgiveness of sins through his name. (Acts.10:34-38)

"Sirs, what must I do to get saved?" They said: "Believe on the Lord Jesus and you will get saved, you and your household." (Acts.16:30, 31) For if you publicly declare that 'word in your own mouth,' that Jesus is Lord, and exercise faith in your heart that God raised him up from the dead, you will be saved. (Rom.10:9; also see Acts.2:36-39, 8:34-39)

Despite the claims of some religious leaders, the good news that saves is simple, and centered on Jesus Christ. It has nothing to do with complicated theological systems or prophetic speculations. That which was sufficient for salvation in the first century, is still sufficient for salvation in the twenty-first. The Christian message has not changed. To suggest otherwise is to subvert Scripture with our own salvation scheme. By focusing on salvation through Jesus Christ, as the Scriptures do, we will be unified in the essential Christian message.

Of course, there is much material in the Bible beyond basic salvation. There are details about God's kingdom, which Jesus proclaimed extensively. There is information regarding the state of the dead and the resurrection. There is practical guidance on daily Christian living and fellowship. There are much Bible prophecies that require diligent study. The Bible encourages us to "call out for understanding", to "keep seeking wisdom as for hidden treasures" (Prov.2:3-4). Christians should have the goal of progressing in their spiritual understanding through serious Bible study and prayer. Gaining a deeper knowledge of God, and His purposes equip a Christian to be a better teacher, able to "bring out of his treasure things new and old". (Matt.13:52)

However, caution is in order. Although Christians should pursue a deeper understanding of Scripture, we should not insist that others adopt our particular view as essential belief—no matter how convinced we are of its truth. We must remember that no one can lay any other foundation than that which is already laid: Jesus Christ is the foundation of our faith. (1Cor.3:11) We should keep in mind the principal: **In essentials unity, in non-essentials freedom, in all things love.** And the essential teachings are focused on Jesus, our Lord and Savior: what he has done and continues to do for us, to the glory of God, the Father.

SUMMARY

For those who are searching for more meaningful Christian fellowship, House Church is a good option. It has its challenges, but the rewards far outweigh the costs. To be a part of a functioning, spirit-led House Church is to be near the heart of Jesus. If you can't find one near you, simply ask a friend or two to come to your home for a meal and some Bible study. Jesus promises to be there. (Matt.18:20) Pray for direction. Pray for each other and for those in need. Sing praise songs. Be patient, empathetic and loving as your group grows and matures. (Phil.2:3) Be unified in biblical essentials, but allow freedom in non-essentials. (Rom.14:5) Experience the peace and joy of worshipping God in true Christian freedom.

Chapter Twenty-One

ORGANISM OR ORGANIZATION?

LM GRANT
By Permission

PART I

Exo.18 has sometimes been used as an argument to justify a practice in the Church of appointing people to certain places of responsibility and dignity, so that operations might proceed more smoothly. Does the Spirit of God have any such intention in recording the advice of Jethro, and Moses accepting this advice without question?

There was a friendly spirit between Jethro and his son-in-law, Moses. Jethro had not shared in the afflictions of Israel in their liberation from Egyptian bondage, but coming to visit Moses afterward, he found Moses sitting from morning till night to hear the cases of Israelites and to pass judgment for them. It was a most plausible alternative he suggested, one that appeals favorably to our natural thoughts. But notice that Jethro said, "I will give you counsel, and God will be with you". (v.19) He did not suggest that God would give Moses counsel, but implied that God would be with Moses, if Moses accepted Jethro's counsel. He advised Moses to appoint able and conscientious men to judge the smaller matters that arose between the people, and they could bring the larger matters to Moses.

Moses evidently considered that this was perfectly logical, and who could quarrel with this? But one fatal flaw was evident in adopting this advice. God had not commanded it, and **Moses did not even consult God about this matter.** Jethro could give the advice, then leave. He had not been linked with Israel in their former afflictions, and he was not to be linked with them in their wilderness trials. Moses chose "to suffer affliction with the people of God", but Jethro did not. (Heb.11:25)

If God intended Moses to act as he was doing, could He not give him strength for it? Certainly He could. But this history illustrates something most serious. Moses is a type of Christ. Should believers be content to have other people settle the problems they consider small, and only bring the great things to the Lord? No! We should go directly to the Lord with every occasion of need. **The introduction of intermediaries is the legal principle of human organization.** No wonder we find God introducing the law of Moses in Exodus 19, and God Himself putting Israel under a form of organization that Peter later spoke of as **"a yoke — which neither our fathers nor we were able to bear."** (Acts.15:10)

But even among Christians, the natural tendency of our hearts is to revert to legal bondage in some way, and we fail to realize that **human organization in the Church of God is legal bondage**. Where some people are put in special places, then others do not need the spiritual exercise of being in the Lord's presence to receive guidance, for they get their guidance from human sources.

The body of Christ, the Church, is not an organization, but an organism, that which is vitally connected to the Head of the body, and which receives its nourishment, guidance and direction from the Head. (Eph.4:15-16) When first instituted after the resurrection of the Lord Jesus, the Church had no human head on earth, such as Moses. Apostles were present, not as being authorities themselves, but as unitedly insisting on the sole authority of the Lord Jesus. When some Jewish believers came to Antioch and insisted that Gentile believers should be circumcised and kept the law, this was settled at Jerusalem, not by the authority of any apostle, but by the word of God, (Acts.15:7-8; 17-18) which was declared by the apostles and accepted by the gathered brethren.

It was necessary to have apostles as the connecting link between the dispensation of law and that of the grace of God, necessary that such men of devoted character should be used to lay the foundation of Christianity, (1Cor.3:10-11; Eph.2:20) that is, to lay down the truth of God concerning Christ in all His relationships. Apostles themselves passed away, but they have left their writings, Scriptures that are authoritative, and by which the Church of God may be guided and preserved in all her subsequent history. While they were living, apostles did appoint elders/bishops in various assemblies, and Paul instructed Titus to appoint elders in each assembly in Crete. (Titus.1:5) Assemblies never did appoint elders, and there are no apostles living to do so now, nor delegates of the apostles.

However, once the Church has been established, there is no reason why believers should not be unitedly guided by the Spirit of God, who remains as a living power in the Church, as it was not true under the dispensation of law. Are there no elders/bishops therefore? By all means elders are still in the Church, but not as appointed by men. There are those who can do the work without any appointment, for God has fitted them for the work. We should certainly pray for such, and appreciate their wise counsel and help.

As far as the ministry of the word of God is concerned, He Himself gives gifts to those who respond to His own leading in devoted service. They do not need the appointment of men, but the power of God. If the assembly sees a spiritual gift in a saint, they should gladly encourage him. With the Spirit of God leading, there will be humility and unity. The assembly will gladly express fellowship with such a servant in the measure in which they can approve of his service.

In all spiritual services, we are therefore to depend, not in any way upon human arrangements, but upon the power of the Spirit of God. On the other hand, in Acts.6:3, the saints at Jerusalem were told to look out from among themselves seven men of good reputation to take care of material needs among the saints. These are the deacons of which 1Tim.3:8-13 speak. As to caring for material things, the assembly is perfectly right to appoint those whom they can trust to do this work. But God does not allow us to choose for ourselves the ministers of spiritual things whom we desire. How good it is that God cares for us so perfectly!

Yet we so little respond to this that when difficulties arise, we look all around us for some human means of meeting these. Such means will be appealing to our rationalizing minds, things that have been adopted by many groups of Christians, but leaving out the clear leading of God by His Spirit. How humbling it is that we are thus expressing the opinion that Christ is not enough!

It is natural to desire a thriving testimony, but if such a testimony becomes an object, then Christ has lost His place as the one Object worthy of our confidence. Let us return to our first love, and value the living power of the Spirit in the body of Christ.

CHURCH'S SCRIPTURES

Eph.1:22, 2:10-22; Eph.4:24;
2Cor.5:17; Gal.2:21-22;
2Cor.5:15-21; 1Cor.10:4;
Col.1:18

The Church cannot send anyone into the Mission Field. If she sends anyone, it will never be by the approval and consent of

God. God sends, before the Church approves, in keeping with the will and purposes of God. Jesus Christ saw the actions and heard the words of His Father before He ever did anything on the earth. Any one thus sent is an Apostles of the Lord.

Jesus Christ; John, the Baptist; the apostles and the prophets of God had to be sent first by God, and the Church must recognize what God has sanctioned. Moses was sent by God to the Hebrews in Egypt. (Exo.3:10) John was sent by God to the Israelites to be His Son's forerunner in preparation for the redemption of humanity. (Jn.1:6) Jesus Christ was sent by His Father to humanity to be the Savior of the world. (Jn.3:16) The apostles, Barnabas and Saul were sent by the Spirit of God to the Gentile world. (Acts.13:2-3) The Scriptures say, **"How can they preach, unless they are sent?"** (Rom.10:15)

God is the Maker, Owner and Creator of the 7.2 billion souls that live on earth today. We did not create ourselves, and we belong to God, the un-created Creator and the un-beginning Beginner. His are the Kingdom, the glory, the honor and the majesty. He owns the earth and the fullness thereof including mankind. (Psm.24:1-2 and 89:11) He is the Boss and Big Kahuna of all from eternity past, present and future. He is the almighty God, and the Possessor of heaven and earth. (Gen.14:19)

If we are sent from man without the previous approval from the Lord, we have no backing from heaven. Many have gone without Him, sending their people into the parts of the world. They were mostly subjected to the constant attack and the confrontation of the evil one. They believed that He sent them when He said, "Go into all the world, and preach the Gospel." (Matt.28:19)

God is the Owner of the people, and they numbered into 7.2 billion souls. The devil wants us to go in the power and authority of humanity, but such misguided venture is met with disasters and calamity. The power of the Holy Spirit should precede the missionaries, apostles, evangelists, prophets, teachers and pastors who must go to home and foreign lands to preach the Gospel.

Just because the Christ says, "Go Ye" does not mean go now. We must go, but we must wait for the green light from the Lord of the harvest. We must seek His face in prayers, intercession and supplications, if we want to be successful in working for the Lord. We must hear a fresh word from heaven before we proceed. He wants to go ahead of us, and we should not live Him behind. If we do the works of God by His instructions, ways and methods, His blessings will be upon us abundantly. There were prophets who presumed upon the Lord in the OT when He has not sent them, neither has spoken to them, but the results were fatal and calamitous. No ambassador goes from his home country without the backing of the government who is sending him.

PART II

Frank L. Preuss
By Permission

This time of the Spirit's presence on earth indwelling the Church, "We are ALL baptized by one Spirit into ONE Body", as well as individually in each believer. (Amazing fact!) The time where there is Christ, the Head (of the body) in heaven; where the Church is not of earthly hopes. (As Israel is and properly should be) But the Church is a heavenly body in Christ in the heavens. (Eph.1)

It may be that the dots are not connected, because it upsets the denominational, vicarious norm of the "Church System" whose roots are (largely) very firmly in earthly things. I do not refer only to the known riches of the Catholic System! This would affect many peoples' pockets!

The practical effect of the presence of the Spirit to guide in the Church without requiring a system and organization of man is unrealized to great a loss, both in response to God, and in effectiveness to the world. Our Lord Jesus Christ and the Spirit of the Father of course, still graciously help and bless wherever saints of God are.

The Church is an organism - not an organization. The Bible pictures the Church as a body of a human being and its members are like members of a human body. One is a foot, one a hand, one an ear, another an eye. The body is a unit, though it is made up of many parts; and though all its parts are many, they form one body. So it is with Christ. (1Cor.12:12) **There is no organization that runs a human body and keeps it alive**. What runs a body and keeps it alive is the spirit, because when the spirit leaves a human body, then this body is dead.

It is the same with the body of Christ - the Church of God. To keep it alive, we need the Holy Spirit. When we start to replace the Holy Spirit with an organization, then the Holy Spirit leaves. The Holy Spirit leaves because He cannot guide the members anymore, because the organization is doing it now. When the believers come together, the individuals are not led any more by the Holy Spirit, but by the organizational forms imposed by the organization. The Holy Spirit is not given any more liberty and He leaves. The moment the Holy Spirit leaves, the Church is dead - spiritual dead.

The key to understand an organism is to see that an organism has only one head. Everything is directed from this head. In the Church of God this head is Jesus Christ. And to understand this main characteristic of an organism - to have only one head - is to understand unity. If every member focuses on Jesus, then we have unity. If certain members start to focus on something else, like men - I follow Peter, I follow Apollos, I follow Paul, I follow Luther, I follow Calvin - or organizations, that are out growing of this urge to follow men - then we have the unity disturbed.

So I am simply in unity with the Christian next to me by being in tune with Jesus. And I am in unity with a Christian on the other side of the world by being in tune with Jesus. It is that simple. When the Christian next to me starts to speak to me, unity is already there - even before he has said the first word. The same with the Christian on the other side of the world, if he writes a letter to me, he is already in unity with me while he is still writing - before I even receive the letter, because he is tuned in to Jesus and I am.

We have to see the difference between an organization and an organism. When we see what the difference is between these two, it will be much easier for us to see the difference between a man-made church and the true Church.

Let us first have a look at an organization. An organization has various links between the top person and the member at the end of the chain of command. At the top you have got the archbishop, the moderator, the pope or whoever the different denominations call their top man. And then you have the next level: bishops, cardinals etc. Another level is dominee, pastor, priest, and reverend. The last person in the chain is the member of that organization.

The whole thing is structured like an army: different officers and at the bottom, the private or airman or sailor. The private talks to his superior officer, let's say to the sergeant. He does not go to the captain to report, he does not go the general, no, he just goes to the immediate superior. If he would report to several levels higher up, the whole organization would not work. It might even kill him, because his direct superior cannot act, because of lacking information. The whole army might even get defeated.

Now let us look at an organism. In an organism, every member is directly linked to the head. In the true Church, every believer is directly reporting to the Lord and is directly led by the Lord. If a believer does not know the Lord, he will be defeated, he will even die, because the Lord does know him and he is therefore not really part of God's family. When it comes to the crucial point in his life, he will be like the five virgins. Jesus said to them "I don't know you." (Matt.25:12)

They had just second hand knowledge of Him. They were dealing with merchants. It is a matter of life and death, not only for the one individual, but for the whole organization - or denomination - he belongs to. Jesus does not know them, because they never had contact with him, because they were always reporting and receiving orders from their denominations and not from Him.

If in an organization, the chain of command is not followed, the organization will be defeated, and many members or even all, might lose their lives. If in an organism, the direct link with the head is not maintained, the same might happen: death.

But the working of an organism is completely different from the working of an organization. The inclination to go for an organization is always preceded by some simple things. These are things like jealousy, pride, love for the things of the world, not recognizing the body of Christ, following men instead of Christ, boasting about men, taking pride in one man over against another. And the result is carnality. And all this follows the urge to form an organization. This urge is also often accompanied by the hope to become somebody important in this organization. And then of course, there are those who want to have their own kingdom, and are instigating the forming of an organization.

Now in order to understand how an organism like the true Church operates, we want to look at examples where members of the body are directly led by the Lord, and are responding to this leading of the Holy Spirit.

Our first example is Ananias in Damascus. The Bible describes Ananias as a disciple. He was not an elder, an apostle or an evangelist. He was just a disciple, but he received direct orders from the Lord. (Acts.9:10-19) The Lord and Ananias discussed the assignment Jesus gave Ananias, and Ananias did what he was told by Jesus. Ananias did not report to the elders of the Church in Damascus, and he did not try to get their blessing or approval. There was no council meeting to discuss if that approach toward the enemy was really the right thing to do or to discuss if Ananias really got instruction from the Lord or if it just was the idea of a zealous Church member.

So a member in the body of Christ has one head and this is Christ himself, there are no others in between. Only a spiritual person will understand this - a person who knows what it means to be led by the Spirit of God, who knows that he is a son of God, because those who are led by the Spirit of God are the sons of God.

Here, it becomes quite clear that there is a connection between being led by God's Spirit and staying away from man-made churches. We will only understand how the true Church works when we also understand the leading of the Spirit, when we understand the problem of jealousy and when we understand the problem of following people. We are discussing here several aspects of Christian life and only when we grasp how interconnected they are, will we start to recognize Jesus and his body.

Let us go to the second example. It is the setting apart of Barnabas and Saul for the work to which the Holy Spirit had called them. (Acts.13:1-4) This setting apart was not done by the Church at

Antioch or by a meeting of prophets and teachers in the Church at Antioch. It was done by the Holy Spirit. The Holy Spirit gave the command. The prophets and teachers did not send them on their way, no, it was the Holy Spirit. In Acts.13:3, the word "apoluo" is used, when it says "they sent them off".

And this "sending" in Acts.13:3 is not that of commissioning, but of letting go, intimating that they would gladly have retained them. In the next verse, in Acts.13:4, we find who commissioned them. The Spirit of God sent them. The word says, "The two of them, being sent on their way by the Spirit, went down to Seleucia and sailed from there to Cyprus". A different word is used this time. This word "sent" (ekpempo) expresses - in contrast to "apoluo" - the act of commissioning by the Holy Spirit.

So, the Spirit of God who was in control and not men, was the One in charge. And contrary to common opinion, the work that Barnabas and Saul did was not controlled by the Church at Antioch. The Church at Antioch did not control their movements, did not tell them what to do, did not finance their trip. All these ideas come up again and again, because people who read the Bible have a certain idea of what the Church looks like, and try to see that picture of a Church in what they read in the book of Acts. And this certain idea of what the Church looks like, comes of course, from the man-made church, they so well know and deal with.

If we understand the difference between an organization and an organism, it will be much easier for us to see the difference between a man-made church and the real Church. When we talk about the name of the Church and point out that the Bible already has given a name to the Church, like "the Way" or "the Church of God", then, we must see this as an indication to identify the real Church. So when a man-made church gives itself a name, let us say "Agape Fellowship", then we know that we most probably are dealing with an imitation church.

But the fact that these people gave themselves a name is an expression of a deeper problem. **They did not see that the true Church is an organism and not an organization.** They could only think in terms of organization, the main reason probably being that all other Christian groups have the form of an organization. So giving a name to a church is very much a sign that we have an organization in front of us.

An organization needs a name. And this name must be official, because it is needed for various purposes. Without a name the "church" cannot exist in the "world". You cannot open an account for a group without a name, you cannot just print the telephone number in the telephone directory without putting a name in front of it. You cannot send the income tax you have to pay for the salary of the pastor and the employees to the receiver of revenue, without giving a name, telling the taxman which "church" sends the money. The name is just one sign of an organization. There are others. An organization has member lists, has members, who represent the organization, has an address, has a telephone number, a tax number, and an office.

And all these things are not found in the real Church - an organism. There is no membership list on this earth - our names are written in the Lamb's book in heaven; it is a spiritual book that cannot be investigated by the police. Our name is a spiritual name - we will not find it in the telephone directory. Our elders are spiritual people without responsibilities and rights described by the laws of the country in which we live. We do not have offices and church buildings and own property, because we meet in homes and our contact with the world is via individual members of the body. If the Church for example handles money, then a certain member or several members will do this and will do everything that is necessary to keep the money or to transfer the money and they will be responsible for the technicalities.

And the Church does not employ people. Elders are people who live a normal working life and in their spare time, do whatever is required. There is no "pastor" - somebody who comes to "pastor" the Church and gets a salary for the services rendered. And there is no regional office and there is no head office and there is no pope and Vatican in Rome, because there is no man between a child of God and God himself. But every child of God is directly in contact with God's Spirit and Jesus Christ.

There is not such a thing that the believer goes to the elder and the elder goes to the bishop and the bishop to the cardinal and he to the pope and the pope is the representative of God on earth.

Elders in the Church - and there is a plurality of elders, there is multiple eldership, not a single "pastor" - are there to prepare God's people for works of service, so that the body of Christ may be built up, until we all reach unity in the faith and in the knowledge of the Son of God, and become mature, attaining to the whole measure of the fullness of Christ. (Eph.4:12-13) The words "until" and "mature" are important in these verses. The elders have a function for the maturing of God's people - they play a role "until" God's people are mature. Because God's people are led by God and not by the elders; the elders are just there to help in this process, but they are not there so that people start to be led by them.

On their mission trip, Barnabas and Saul appointed elders for them in each Church. (Acts.14:23) That was when they returned to Lystra, Iconium and Antioch. But before that, they had established these Churches. So the establishment of Churches comes before the appointing of elders. The establishment of Churches was the decisive thing, not the appointment of elders. And from this report we also can see that Churches can very well exist without the Church planter remaining present. There was a new Church, probably just a few weeks old, and the two men who brought this Church into life left.

And this Church carried on existing as if nothing had happened, because these Christians received their life from the Holy Spirit, and not from men. And Churches can exist without elders, because after Barnabas and Saul had left and before they came back, there were no elders. So there was this brand new Church and no apostles and no elders. And these Christians just kept on growing, because they received their life directly from the head of the Church. They were taught to have a direct relationship with the Creator of the universe - and that was more than enough.

When we have a Church, then we put our trust in God to run this Church. This is one meaning of trusting God: not to put our trust in anybody else - also not in ourselves - only God. We actually distrust ourselves. We distrust ourselves and do not try to lead the local Church; we leave it to God.

So we have to understand these things. Elders are not the people who guide and run the Church, and elders are not the people who guide and run the Church meeting. The Holy Spirit does these things through the Church. And especially elders don't run the meetings. There is no such thing that there is only one elder - a "pastor" - who has a one-man show on Sunday morning.

But now you might say, "Are we not supposed to submit to elders?" Yes, we are. But this submitting is the same as when I submit to a brother, or I submit to the worldly authority. If the traffic light is red, then I stop and wait until it becomes green. I submit to the rules of the authority, but it does not mean that these authorities run my life. If a brother, and it might be a brother that is very young in the Lord, corrects me, then I submit to him and I even do it if a non-Christian says something to me from which I can deduct that he is indirectly pointing out a short coming in my behavior.

When Christians come to you with this submitting business, that every Christian has to submit to another Christian, ask them to whom was Martin Luther supposed to submit? And insist that they give you an answer. The only person we allow to control us is the Lord. And this we do voluntary, we actually work at it that the Lord takes over more and more aspects of our lives. We give up more and more of the throne we have sat on before we made Him Lord of our lives. When we say that Jesus is our Lord, then we also say that nobody else is our boss, not we ourselves, but also no other man. Submitting is an act of admitting that the other person made a suggestion that is right - spiritual right.

But I submit to another's suggestion voluntary, not because others have the right to tell me what to do. Paul was an apostle to those who wanted his apostleship, because they realized his spirituality. Christian who did not think that Paul had these qualities simply did not receive him and Paul did not try to force himself upon them. Still today, we can read Paul's letters and do what he suggests or leave it. I can tell somebody what to do and it is up to him to accept the advice or to ignore it. That is the difference between the kingdoms of light and that of darkness. The devil will always try to deceive us in order to gain control over us, and when he gets control over someone, then, he puts that person into bondage. (Bondage of death - not of life)

So we are led by the Lord and not by elders. When we study elders, we will find that the emphasis is more on what elders are, than on what elders do. In Titus.1:5-9 and 1Pet.5:1-4, we find lists of characteristics of elders and little what they are supposed to do. The important thing of an elder is to be like Christ. The doing is probably best described in Titus.1:9 "to encourage others".

The real Church is an organism or a very strange organization. An organism with two and half members, and Christ is the only One Leader. And all members report to this One Leader and this Leader knows all the members, and knows them very intimately. He knows their hearts. Here again we can see that such a thing is only possible because it is a spiritual "entity". It is an "entity" run in a supernatural way. Only a spiritual person will be able to understand and to accept such a set up.

A carnal person - a person that does not understand how a person can be led by the Holy Spirit, will have problems seeing how it can be possible to not have a spiritual entity, called the Church. They do not really believe God. They do not really believe that God is almighty. That He can know millions and millions of Christians, and that He can even lead them all individually at the same time. That He can deal with millions of different aspects of his kingdom at one moment. He deals with every one of them individually. He controls every detail of their individual lives, whether spiritually or physically.

So there is one body and one head. The head of the Church that meets in a house is the Lord, and the head of all the Churches in different houses in a town is also the Lord, and the head of all the Churches of several towns of one region is also the Lord, and the head of all the Churches in a country is the Lord, and the head of all the Churches in the world is the Lord. This is not an organization. It is an organism, like the organism of a human body - only one head.

And all the direction we receive is from our head, the Lord. And because we are led by the Lord, that is why we are not independent of the other members, and that is why we are in unity.

We do not follow men and we do not follow organizations. And we do not have men as our masters. We do not have organizations as our masters. Jesus defined this explicitly in Matt.23:8, "You have only one Master, and you are all brothers". We have only one Master and we cannot serve two masters. We cannot serve the Lord and an organization. If we are devoted to an organization, we will despise the Lord. So we only can hate an organization and love the Master. There is no compromise.

PART III

The Church is alive. She is the Bride of Christ. She is Christ's Body. We are living stones. We are living organism. The Church must be left alone to be the organism, and she will be, and will not be made into an organization.

An organization is dead. An organization is like a business. An organization is legislated. An organization can be mapped out, can be written out, and planned out. It is something to be observed on a chalkboard or in a textbook. An organism on the other hand, is alive, evolving, unpredictable, ever changing, and constantly growing. An organism such as the Church is not to be measured, contrived, pre-determined, calculated or controlled, but rather it is to be lived and experienced.

Let's look at a wild animal for example. Let's take an eagle. An eagle can spread its wings and fly. It can fly wherever it wants to, and it can fly however fast it wants to. It can fly as high as it wants to fly. It can hunt whatever it wants to hunt. It can hunt when it wants to hunt and where it wants to hunt. This beautiful and organic creature can soar to the highest mountaintops. From the high mountain peaks, it can spot its prey hundreds of feet below, and then dive with extreme accuracy to snatch its food from the tiny stream at the bottom.

What if we took this glorious and organic creature and put it in a cage? What if we provided its food for it, so it would not have to hunt anymore? That would be nice and helpful, but the animal would not want that. And then, what if we scheduled when it was to eat? What if we also limited where it could go? Yes, in fact, we shall build for it a big beautiful building to live in. It will be large, magnificent, and expensive. It will be such a beautiful sanctuary!

Perhaps organic things should not be allowed to roam so free and wild. We should contain them so they will have a proper diet, exercise, and environment to thrive in. We should even hire trained professionals to feed and care for the bird. Because of our modern wisdom and education, we have learned what is best for the eagle. We have become experts. The eagle will be much better off in our institutional care than in the care of its natural habitat.

In the above situation, would our eagle still be an eagle? Of course, technically, it would still be an eagle. But it would not thrive. It would not live and be how it was intended to live and be. Soon, our magnificent eagle with wither, deteriorate and lose heart. It will not function properly as it should. And by our trying to help it, and enjoy it for ourselves, all we have done is helped it to weaken. Structuring and organizing a living organic thing will stifle, and could even kill it.

The Church is just like an eagle. We try to help her by containing her, packaging, and over structuring her. We stifle her growth and cause people to lose heart.

Most people have never seen a wild eagle doing what it does in its natural habitat. We only read about wild eagles. The same is true for the Church. Very few have ever seen the Church functioning in her natural state and at her full potential. We only read about her in the New Testament.

It is because we have put the Church in a cage. What are some things that structure, the living Church organism, and cause her to be an organization? And how does this man made structuring hinder and stifle us?

The Churches in the New Testament did not have names. They

were only referred to according to the city they were in. Giving a name to a group is probably the biggest thing that changes the Church into an organization. (Refer to "One Church in a City") With a name, we create an identity that is separate from others, thus we change the organism into an organization. A checking account, a Church bulletin, a board of directors, by-laws, and documented membership lists are all things that create an organization. There are many more things that can do this as well.

Erroneously, there is a very strong need in men to legislate the Church. Men want to identify her, categorize her, and organize her, using modern Western ways. Instead of just allowing the living Church organism to just be whatever she is, men want to be able to get their hands on her, so she can be manipulated, easily identified, and managed.

> Why can't we just be people who love Jesus Christ, and are spending time together?

OUR NEED FOR AN ORGANIZATION

The answer is found in the word security, having, and being able to count on some things. There is not much security in a lose network of Christians who are just spending lots of time together, without a name, without a building, without a regular meeting time, and without a membership list. Who would we be in such a case? What would our identity be? The answer is, we would simply be the people of God. Our name would be "the Church of whatever city we happen to be in" (the Church in Sacramento, the Church in Pasadena, the Church in Boston, the Church in New York, the Church in Winnipeg, the Church in Vancouver etc.

Others would know us, and who we are by our intense love for one another, our practice of close community living, and our constant good works. However, we have resorted to other, more modern ways to allow ourselves to know who we are, to let other people know who we are, and to be able to survive and increase our membership. This is contradictory to the will of God.

If you belong to a lose network of Christians who have no legislation, no identifiable name, and who are not an organization, you have nothing that your flesh can count on. With a loose network of relationships that is not packaged, branded, and boxed, there is not much of a feeling of having something you can control or belong to.

First of all, we must begin to understand that the Church does not belong to us. Nor does she exist for us. She does not belong to a leader or to any man. The Church belongs to Jesus Christ. We exist for Him.

Men want to have something. Men want to build something. Many times, your pastor-type-people want to build their own kingdoms, and say they are building God's Kingdom. If it were truly God's Kingdom, they were building, they would do it His way, and restrict themselves to only New Testament practices, and leave the building up to Jesus Christ. Instead of being so concerned with growing it, building it, and managing it, men should get their hands off the Church. If there is no membership list, no clearly identifiable line of those who belong to "us" and those who don't, then the people in leadership don't get to experience the feeling of having something to possess and build that is their own.

When we take the organic, living, spontaneous, relationship driven Church and formally organize it, thus making it an organization, we kill much of the life and potential for growth. Groups ponder and question all the time how they can grow closer to one another, have more intimacy with one another, and have more spontaneity, yet they continue to depend on a modern system of organization to keep them together.

Let me explain how this works and why it is so detrimental: Cathy has a need. She needs someone in the Church to help her do some yard work. In an organization, all she has to do is tell the pastor. He will then approve the need to go into the Church bulletin. Anyone who wants to help can then be notified. On the surface, this would seem like a very efficient and effective method of communication. It maybe an efficient system of communication; however, it will kill multiple opportunities for spontaneity, for relationships, and for intimacy.

Let's look how this particular need would be communicated and met with only a living organism of relationships, instead of an organization. When Cathy feels the need for some help in doing the yard work, she picks up the phone and calls someone. Or, she can make a couple of visits in person to some people who are closest to her in her life. Cathy says to a family while standing in their kitchen, "Hey, I could really use some help with my yard. Could you all maybe find the time to help out sometime?"

What just happened in Cathy's situation? What does this personal, one-on-one asking accomplish when done in person? What does it accomplish, that a posting in a bulletin on Sunday, would not accomplish? It accomplishes plenty of things. If she communicates her need in person and through relationships only, Cathy gets to have conversations with people. She gets to ask with a vulnerable heart. She gets to stay over for 30 minutes and have a glass of tea. She gets prayed for. She gets to experience someone's heart on the other end of the conversation. The family that she asks gets to see her and hear her heart. They get to experience her real need as she communicates it as a real person. The people she asks gets to let Cathy know of some needs that they've been experiencing as well.

The family she is asking also gets prayed for by Cathy. The family she is asking, in turn gets to ask Cathy if she will watch their kids while they go on a date for the evening. All sorts of great things happen when we deal with one another person to person, face to face and often. Efficient systems and organization tend to separate us from one another. The Church will have order, but it will evolve naturally from within.

Let's look at another example. It is Tuesday afternoon. John and Sharon are hungry for some fellowship. They would both really love to have people over to their house tonight. However, there is a scheduled meeting on the following night, which will be on Wednesday. They decide to go ahead and wait until Wednesday to get with people, because in the Church Organization they belong to, they would have to notify the leadership and then announce the gathering at their house on the Church's website. Also, typically the way things work in their group, people like to plan things a week or so in advance.

Let's look at the same situation, but let's see how it might occur in only an organism or relationships, instead of an organization. John and Sharon are feeling a need for some fellowship. John and Sharon would then pick up the phone and start making calls that very afternoon. The people they fellowship with are used to spontaneous invitations all of the time. Usually about half of the people they call will probably show up. Many will change their current plans or modify their plans, in order to be with the saints tonight. It doesn't matter to anyone that there is a regularly scheduled meeting the following night. Many acknowledge the Lord in the invitation.

Apparently, the Lord was really moving in John and Sharon when they felt the need to get the saints together on this particular Tuesday night. Sharon had a really big cry in her that she was unaware of because of some recent difficulties she was having at work. She really needed some counsel and some prayer. A new sister that no one had ever met before also showed up to John and Sharon's house that night. Several people ministered to the new sister with prayer and by talking through some things. The new sister would not have been able to make the Wednesday meeting on the following night. There was tremendous joy at John and Sharon's house that night, because the people who came, came because they wanted to, not because they had to. Many were so blessed that John and Sharon would personally call them and invite them to their home.

Just think what it would be like if there were no formal man made organization, no system in place to take care of us, no fabricated structure for people to look to and depend on, nothing at all artificial to gather us together, to communicate needs, to make announcements, to tell us where to be, no organization to tell us who we are, when to pray, or when we could meet – but all that we had were relationships to accomplish all of these things. How closely knit and intimate we would become! Just think how many more spontaneous and intimate opportunities we would have to be joined together.

With only relationships to bring us together, what you wind up with is – relationships. With no organization to run the show and to automatically keep things going, you get prayed for and loved on much more often. There are also more real opportunities to serve and bless others. Intimacy, vulnerability and closeness come through much time, and much person-to-person interaction. If we are relating to an organization, instead of one another, it will contribute to keeping us apart.

An organization is an artificial method to keep us together, and maintain continuity that ends up killing the life within. Let's take another example. Griner is not in leadership in his Church. However, Griner loves to study the Scriptures and he really has a heart for the growth of the other people in his fellowship. He is feeling stirred to share a teaching with the other members in his congregation. The Lord gave him this message only two days ago. He really senses that the other people he is with need to hear this message. He tells the leadership that he wants to share a message with the group. Since he is not a designated leader, the leadership wants to talk to him first in order to see if the message "fits with what the Lord is doing in the Church". Really they want to screen the message (but they would never use the word "screen")

Because of scheduling conflicts, it takes about a week for the leader(s) to set up the meeting with Griner. About a week later, they do get together and have a chat. The designated leader(s) feel like the message will be OK to share. And, they don't want to say "no," because they don't want to be accused of being controlling. Currently, because the leadership is in the middle of a teaching series, Griner needs to wait to share his message. Griner actually shares the message three weeks later.

When it comes to the time for Griner to actually speak, the message is not quite as fresh in his heart as it used to be. He speaks mostly from memory of what the Lord was showing him almost a month ago, as opposed to what the Lord is showing him now. At the very moment he finished the message, the leadership stood up and took back control of the meeting. There were also a couple of subtle comments made by the leadership to the audience of how they disagreed on a minor point.

It was pretty clear to Griner that the leadership in the Church was more or less "permitting" him to share the message, instead of really wanting and desiring him to share it. The way the whole thing came down and the vibe he got from the leadership was not extremely encouraging. In the future, Griner will not be quite as eager to dig in the Scriptures in order to share teachings with the group.

Let's look at the same scenario, but within a New Testament environment. What if there were only a living organism of relationships to govern it and not an organization?

Griner would feel stirred to preach a message to the saints. Immediately, he would bounce it off a few available brothers

– any available brothers. He would then call the saints on the phone, or he would go visit each family to tell them about the teaching time and when it was. He would then share the message in a matter of days, full of the Spirit, with plenty of unction, in God's timing, and in total freedom.

Toward the end of the message, Griner felt impressed to pray for different people regarding the message he spoke. The message also inspired others to stand up and share testimonies. One young man stood up and confessed a sin. There was tremendous freedom and an atmosphere of healing in the group. Many were blessed and there were multiple breakthroughs that occurred.

Man's systems of organization dictate to us who is speaking, when they are speaking, and if they get to speak at all. The example of leadership we see in religious organizations is leadership by control, not facilitation. The gifts among us are often stifled and discouraged. In religious organizations, we are often given teachings on how we should be an active, and functioning members. We are taught and encouraged to operate and function in our gifts, but then when we do, it is discouraged, frowned upon, or stifled.

Here's another example. Frank Parker has a cousin coming to visit him from out of town. It's his younger cousin, Mark Parker. Mark just received his degree from Bible College. Mark is very excited to share his new knowledge he has learned in Bible College to a group of believers somewhere. Mark Parker asks his cousin Frank if he could share at the men's group meeting that Frank is regularly a part of. Frank asks his pastor if it is OK for Mark to speak at the men's meeting. Frank's pastor tells him "No, it probably wouldn't be best for Mark to speak at this time." Frank's pastor is personally aware that the Bible College cousin Mark graduated from is not really sound in doctrine. Conveniently, there are other things planned for the evening men's meeting anyway.

Let's look at this situation and how it would have came down within an organism of New Testament relationships only: Cousin Mark shows up from out of town. He wants to share at the men's meeting Frank is a part of. He did not have to get permission. It is an open meeting. There was not even a designated person to get permission from. He begins to share at the meeting. He begins to share unsound doctrine. After he speaks for a while, an older brother in the meeting politely interrupts him. "Excuse me Mark.

We sure do appreciate your willingness to share with us. But some of the points and topics you are covering are not exactly how the Lord has shown us to view and relate to those particular Scriptures. In other words brother, your faith is not the same as ours concerning those issues. Would it be OK with you, if you and I talked about some of the topics you are bringing after the meeting time?" Cousin Mark replies, "Sir, what Scriptures are you referring to specifically?" The older brother explains, "Well brother, again, would it be OK with you if we discussed it at a separate time?"

Cousin Mark finally gets the point. He humbles himself, agrees, and enjoys the rest of the meeting. Or, Cousin Mark may get offended, get real quite for a while, and then walk out of the meeting. The point is that everyone gets an opportunity to observe something, and to learn. The younger brothers felt protected by the older men. They don't need a system or a hierarchy to protect them, but proper relating and functioning protect the Church. Cousin Mark gets a choice to be a humble man, to learn and to grow – or he can be offended – and everyone will get to learn by his bad example. Frank, Mark's older cousin, gets to humble himself as well. He gets to appreciate and respect the older brother who did such a good job of checking Mark. They grow closer in their relationship because of it.

In the above example, the identity of the group is strengthened. What they believe and the direction the Lord is taking them in is more affirmed, but not by an artificial system. In New Testament body life, there is no comparison as to the intimacy and closeness of relationships that you have, and the growth that occurs as opposed to when an organization is present. As I go and visit religious organizations, the people tend to be distant and separate from one another. They' have been trained to be that way. There is a system in place that keeps them apart. A system or an organization is pure legislation. Legislation kills most spontaneity. Legislation stifles deep relationships. Legislation hinders many opportunities for growth.

Some may say, "It is actually organization and legislation that brings us together and keeps us together. Without any organization, we would not ever meet or get together." This is probably true for many groups. If you drop your methods and systems of organization however, you will get to see what you really have. Without methods of organization in place, if no one gets together or pursues one another, you really didn't have much in the first place. People were probably coming out of obligation or religious reasons.

The problem is that people depend and fall back on the system of organization to gather them together, provide teaching, provide music, provide activities and programs, and to keep out false teaching. This promotes passivity in the people. With no system in place to run things, it is up to each member to function and be active in heart – which brings more life, more growth, more learning, and much more quality. You have to risk the very thing you are afraid of.

Traditional Churches are full of religious people who just want God's approval by belonging to the club and attending the club's meetings and functions. They don't really want true, meaningful, deep relationships with others, or with God. They just want to do the minimum requirements necessary to cover their base. If you remove the organization that enables them in this behavior, you will see what you really have. Jesus did things to expose the game players all of the time.

An organization tends to replace relationships. People relate to the organization rather than each other. People belong to the organization, instead of each other. People depend on the organization, instead of only depending on the Lord with each other. People give their money to the organization, instead of giving to each other. People invite others to be a part of their organization, instead of inviting others into their lives. People invest in and build up the organization, instead of investing in and building up one another.

The organization is often an idol, a "golden calf" in the hearts of its members. If you currently belong to a religious organization, it would be extremely rare to not hold at least some degree of affinity or allegiance in your heart towards your organization. If you threaten people's organizations, or talk bad about them, the people who belong to them feel threatened themselves. People have invested their time, their money, their hearts and their lives into building the organization. They do not know how to be, how to belong, or how to function with one another, apart from the organization, or denomination.

Within an organization, members wonder and ponder how to have more intimacy with the Lord and with one another. So erroneously, they organize a meeting to be held in three weeks and post it in the Church Bulletin in order to discuss how to have more intimacy. We are addicted to systems. Systems that continually pull the rug right out from under us with what we are trying to accomplish in the first place.

While many are trying to pursue closer and deeper relationships with the Lord, and with each other, because they belong to and are relating to an organization, it keeps them from being thrown together in spontaneous ways throughout the week.

Think about it like this. Imagine if you lived in a neighborhood of people with no cars, no phones, and no televisions. You would be forced to naturally relate to, talk to, and communicate with the people in your neighborhood. You would be dependent on one another in many ways for survival. This is currently a true situation for most villages on the planet. Just think how close you would become to the others who lived around you. You would have to get off your couch and go visit someone to borrow a cup of milk, instead of using the car. You would have to round up people and ask for help with various tasks and projects.

In the evenings, you would tend to be together with your neighbors, sitting around, and visiting while watching the kids play, instead of watching TV by yourself in the evening. A few ladies might work together during the day to create meals for their families.

What do we currently have in our modern day and age? Instead of deep relationships with our neighbors, we don't really need anyone. We have cars, phones and televisions. Because of our lust for convenience and entertainment, these things have largely replaced the need for one another. Some may say that cars and phones have brought us closer together. But, cars and phones have only made us busier and more spread out. We probably know more people and have more relationships, because of the modern conveniences, but our many relationships are now much shallower and we spend less quality time with individuals. Without cars and phones, we would be stuck with just a few, but the quality and depth would be greater.

I am not against technology or modern conveniences. But, just like cars, phones, and televisions are conveniences that actually contribute to more shallow relationships and busier lives; we have done the same with the Church. We believe that it is much more convenient and efficient to have systems of committees, schedules, bulletins, agendas, boards of directors, treasurers, CEO/Pastor, etc. We are convinced that these things help us, but they do not. We run the Church like it was a business. This costs us the very thing we are trying to accomplish. Life together in Jesus! The typical Church structure is not much different from a typical business structure you will find in corporate America. If you compared say, Exxon's Corporate Structure with your average Church Organization, you would see some amazing similarities.

Again, in a New Testament body life Church, there will be organization. But it will happen naturally and organically. In a living organism of relationships, organizing can be done, but it will be accomplished through relationships and through personal interaction.

FORMS SHOULD BE CREATED FROM THE INSIDE OUT

I am going to get a little theoretical here, but hang with me. It's important for our understanding. We must always let the form of something take its shape from the life within itself. The form is never to be created first or sought after first. For example, an apple does not have the same form as an orange. An apple takes the form that it has, because of the life within itself. It is in the DNA, if you will, of the apple that causes it to look like and take the outward form of an apple. The DNA of a banana causes it to take the outward form of a banana. Some bananas are a little bigger, some a little shorter, and some a little wider than others. The life that is within each banana causes it to take the shape that it does. The amount of nutrients it gets from the soil, the health of the banana tree it came from, and the amount of rainfall and sunshine all dictate the form the banana will take. The life within causes the form to take the shape that it does.

The same is true of any living thing. Some dogs are bigger than others, because some dogs receive a better diet, some get more exercise, and some have a different heredity. The life within causes the outward form to be whatever it is. The outward container becomes what it is, because that particular container happens to be what is needed to support the life within.

The same should be true for the Church. The Church is a living organism. The life within her should cause her outward form to take shape. We should never predetermine the outward form ahead of time. It will kill and squelch what she would have turned out to be naturally. To assume up front what something will look like will hinder it. To establish the form ahead of time will deny it of the natural form it would have taken otherwise. For example, you may have ten families who are sharing life together in the Lord.

Four families out of the ten, may need plenty of time getting to know other people because they are new and don't know anyone. Because of this, these four families will naturally and organically have it in their hearts to spend plenty of time visiting, talking and sharing with others. They may need many hours together telling stories from the past, asking questions of one another, and comparing notes on different subjects with one another. Three families out of the ten may already know each other well, but the Lord is leading them into a season of praying for personal needs for one another. They will want to get together to pray. They will not be talking together quite as much as the first four families are. Still, there may be a couple of families out of the ten who are really focusing outwardly with ministry and who want to spend a lot of their time together in order to help needy people in the community who need extra clothing and shoes.

Within these ten different families, the varying activities will look a certain way, if it is allowed to be what it is and not controlled. It will take a certain form naturally. There will be different nights of the week when various gatherings take place. Some will be for talking. Some will be for prayer. Some will be for sorting through clothing. There will be various get-togethers with a variety of emphasis. If you were to look at these ten families from the outside, the form and the way they look will take their shapes out of the various Spirit led activities that are happening. The form will not be a cookie cutter form that is patterned after every traditional Church Organization on every corner in every city. That would be forcing something that is not natural or organically grown.

An organic form allows the life within it to express itself in the most effective way it can. The form takes the shape that it does in order to allow the life within to express itself adequately. If we were to pre-determine what nights of the week these ten families were to get together on and what they were to do when they got together, it would squelch the life and the very little of what God would want to accomplish would never be accomplished. In fact, as the Spirit brought up various things in the hearts of the families, they would tend to discount them, because they would get used to not expressing the gifts they have.

An organic, natural flowing form takes it shape, because of the needs of the people and because of the desires God puts in their hearts. Every group is different. Every season is different. There are different people in every group with different gifts, different needs, and who are all in different seasons. These things may change every few months. The needs and desires "from the inside out" should dictate the form and what it looks like.

An organic New Testament Church lives from the inside out, not the outside in. If you dictate and legislate who gets together, when they get together and what they do when they get together, you will kill most of what could happen that would be so wonderful. Most Christians have never had the privilege of experiencing Church life in a free flowing, uncontrolled setting. Remember, even an extremely lose and well structured man made organization is still an organization. Men must get their hands completely off the Church. Let her be. Let her thrive and do what she does best. Let the Spirit of God dictate what the Church looks like, in every city, in every gathering. The Church belongs to Jesus Christ. Let it take whatever form she needs to take. Let the needs of the members, the life within, and the passions within the hearts of the people form the structure. A healthy organism will grow and change. The structure must be allowed to grow, change and evolve with the organism. It will look different all of the time. Only a structure that is formed organically, will adequately support, carry and deliver the needs and direction the organism wants to go in.

Over the years, the people I've walked with have expressed themselves in various forms. It always looks the difference from season to season.

It is kind of hard to describe this. But for example, some months we have had a regular meeting time on Saturday night and a regular prayer time on Tuesdays. Everything else during the week was spontaneous. Then a few months later, we will shut down the Saturday meeting and have a Friday night meeting with an emphasis on worship and singing. Then after a while, when it seemed as though the Lord was finished with that, we would have no regular meetings at all for a few months. People will just gather together spontaneously. A brother might call a spontaneous one time teaching for a certain night of the week, a family may open their home for prayer on a particular night.

We may all have a cookout with only a two days advance notice. There may be a ski trip planned with a four months notice. There may be a season where there are pockets of people gathering for different reasons. A few sisters may gather regularly to talk and pray together to learn how to love their kids better. A few men may gather together regularly to learn about finances. A couple of families may meet together to read and study a book together. All of this is sprinkled heavily with plenty of evening suppers together, lunches, and spontaneous prayer times.

There are a myriad of different forms that may take place if you allow the life within to dictate the form. Nothing is dead. No one comes because they have to. Nothing is religious. And no meeting is ever exactly the same. Jesus said that He would build His Church. Let's trust Him to do it the way He wants to.

Chapter Twenty-Two

THE PROGRESSION OF THE CHURCH

LEADERSHIP
(THE PROGRESSION)

Those who failed to learn from history are doom to repeat it. We have human history as well as divine. The human history effects humanity, but God's affect both here and heaven. We have to look at the history of the early Church from the book of Acts and go back to check her out through what Jesus Christ left for her to pass on to us.

JESUS CHRIST

His Ministry: Mk.15:40-41, Matt.27:55-56 Women served Christ out their own pockets and ministered to Him. He went to where people were in the Temple, in the house, people went to Him in an open field, in one or groups of two or more. He was not here to erect a huge cathedral and gathered humanity into it. That is what we do in the 21st century.

He had His last supper in a house called the Upper Room and His disciples met with Him here. Matt.26:17-18, Mk.14:12-16 and Lk.22:7-13. The house was borrowed from the owner. He did not come to this world to impress people about His skills in architecture. He had a mandate from His Father and it was the home coming of the people of God in redeeming them for the Father's glory and honor.

He was found in Jairus' house, in Peter's home, at Zaccheaus abode, Simon, the leper residence, and so many houses. He preached in the Temple and called it, His Father's House, but it was not His favorite place because the Jews sought to kill Him.

At His death, the veil of the Temple that kept the holiest place from the general populace was rent into two from top to bottom, signifying the exit of the Spirit of God. (Matt.27:51) You will never hear Christ raising funds or collecting money to build physical structures. Neither did He advocate for a building to be used for the worship of God, let alone pressurizing the people to give money in order that the Kingdom of God may advance. (Jn.4:24)

The Apostles and Services: The Spirit of God came upon them in a house called the Upper Room, not in a structure, a mega Church building, a glass cathedral or in the Temple. This was the beginning and birth of the Church. (Acts.2:1-11)

Acts.2:41-47: The Church grew from 120 to 3,000, and the Upper Room could not contain them. They were meeting in homes and in groups from house to house. You never heard them soliciting funds for a physical building, but to help the saints around in Jerusalem and elsewhere. The funds the Church gave are for the poor, strangers, orphans, widows and the needy amongst them. They are not for what we use them for in this 21st Century. They did not major in physical building, designated as worship centers.

Acts.3:1-9: Peter and John went into the Temple to pray, because they had scheduled a time of meeting with God, but not for long. The religious leaders wanted their heads in a charger.

Acts.4:1-10: The Sanhedrin, which was both political and religious leaders of the land, forbade them from speaking the Name of Jesus Christ. The Apostles were arrested and summoned before the council. But before the arrest, 5,000 were added to the Church and it grew to 8,120 souls. 120, 3,000 and 5,000 will give us 8,120. If they were in today's world, they will be looking for a large structure that will accommodate them. In today's world, we are always looking for a land to build a mega structure, but before then, the Church met in houses.

The population of the city of Winnipeg is over 1 million souls, and yet there are physical structures and mega building designated as worship centers all over it. The saints of God at this starting point were 8,120, and it was not addition, but multiplication, and the author believed that the Church grew to 16,240 souls. Yet they had no physical building that took the focus away from God. (Acts.6:1) We are not even a third of that number, and we have proliferations of Church structures in Winnipeg. There must be something wrong. The heart of man is the same as it was then, but we have much people and money in today's world. Ours is the world of power, prestige, fame, beauty and greed.

Acts.4:23-31: They went to their own company and reported all that the Chief Priests and the Elders had said and done to them. Where was this company? In the homes of the saints, and it was filled with the glory of God, in so much that it shook to the foundations. (vv.32-37) They had one mind, one spirit and one voice. There were no denominations and no mega structures. They did not worry about hydro bills, heating bills, overheads and all kinds of man-made things that cost money.

Acts.5:14-16: The Church was growing and God was multiplying them. Multitudes of men and women were brought into the Church and the Kingdom of God was growing with amazing rapidity. God wrought special miracles through Peter to the extent that his shadow was healing people as they walked by.

The atmosphere was supercharged with the presence of the Spirit of God and the keepers of the Temple were furious with them.

Acts.6:1-8: The multiplication continued and it brought such a huge number of souls into the Kingdom of God. There were internal problems and the answer to this problem was the choice of 7 men who were called Deacons. They were to serve tables. The house-to-house meeting of the Church was going on, and the Apostles never once worried for a place that could hold 17,000 to 20,000 converts. Amazing! They had houses and homes in which they met.

Acts.7: Stephen recounted the story of how the Hebrew Nation began and the Lord God was at the center of it all. It started with God calling Abraham out from his country and people. Then he had a son, called Isaac and Isaac had Jacob and Jacob had the 12 patriarchs. That was how God began with one man, and made millions of them to form a Nation. God wanted to do the same for the Church and filled the whole world with His people. This ideal in the mind of God was on for the first 100 years, but it quickly changed when men noticed the power and the money that could come out of it.

The saints of God began to erect buildings that took the personality, form and the name of the Church, and this gave rise to the mega buildings, physical structures, glass cathedrals of the modern world. But the Church of God met in homes and houses of the saints. Contrary to the mega Churches of today, the words of the Lord stood opposed to our world. He said, "Fear not little flock, it is your Father's pleasure to give you the Kingdom." (Lk.12:32) **God does not dwell in the temple built by human hands. (Acts.7:44-50)** This should give us a clue as to what we do with structures that we have built to ourselves.

Acts.8: Persecution kept the Church on the move and thus fulfilled Acts.1:8. Philip was forced to go into Samaria and preached Christ unto them. God's Spirit fell amidst signs, wonders and miracles. Peter and John were sent from Jerusalem and the Samarian Saints received the Spirit like Peter and John in Jerusalem. (Acts.2)

Philip did not build a mega structure to house God's people. They met in the houses of the saints and God took care of them all. Meanwhile, Philip was relieved of his duties in Samaria to go to the desert to meet the Minister of Finance, a eunuch, under Queen Candace of Ethiopia. God will always reveal Himself to anyone who is looking for Him. Also, God can take care of His Church, without Philip, and His Church in the city of Winnipeg will go on. The converts in Samaria followed the example of the Church in Jerusalem, meeting from house-to-house without a mega building or a large physical structure.

Acts.9:1-6: Persecution continued to disperse the Church, and as they ran for their dear lives, they were speaking the Word of God. There was a Church that met in the house of Ananias and many such groups in the city of Damascus. (v.10) Christ arrested Saul, the murderer and turned him into a preacher of righteousness by having Ananias go to Saul, who has been fasting for three days. Ananias laid hands on Saul, and he was filled with the Spirit of God as well as received his sight. Something like scales fell from his eyes, and he saw perfectly.

God turned Satan's friend around, who used to be a murderer and one who persecuted His Church, and made him His leading man. Saul began fighting on the Lord's sight, and plundering the kingdom of darkness. The Jews plotted to take his life, but he escaped by night through a basket let down on the walls of the city in a window. His crime was that, "He was preaching Jesus Christ to them as the Savior and Redeemer of the human race. The Lord made Ananias to know that Saul would suffer many things for His Name's sake.

Jesus Christ put a calling upon a murderer and made him a

saint. Only God can do just that, and His grace takes the Ted Bundies, Jack, the reaper and Jim Jones of this world and turns them into His own special people. Saul was a chosen vessel of the Lord to bear His Name before the Gentiles, kings and the children of Israel in this order. (vv.15-16)

Saul escaped to Jerusalem, and tried to join the disciples there, but they refused his entrance, because they were afraid of him. But Barnabas took him and brought him before the Apostles, sharing how the Lord had met and spoken to him, and he saw the Lord in the Spirit. The Apostles accepted the words of Barnabas, because he was credible and they believed him. Saul went in and out amongst them, and Jerusalem was calm relatively. But no sooner had the Jews the knowledge of him who was once their champion. Immediately, they sought to kill him, because he switched side from them to Jesus Christ. They would not have such a fellow, and they called for his head. Saul was shipped to Tarsus, his hometown, and there was rest for the saints briefly.

The Church was born in Samaria and many house Churches were meeting in homes. (Acts.8) The Church was born in Ethiopia through the eunuch and many home Churches were meeting in the country of Ethiopia. (Acts.8:26ff) The Church was born in Azotus region, and many home Churches were meeting in Azotus and the surrounding. (Acts.8:40)

The Church was born in Damascus and one of saints in the city was Ananias. The Church was meeting in the homes of the saints in Damascus. (Acts.9:10) The Church was in the house of Judas, where Saul was staying before Ananias prayed for him to be filled with the Spirit, and healed of his blindness. (Acts.9:11)

The Church was in the homes of the saints at Lydda where Peter prayed for Aeneas and he was healed of paralysis. (Acts.9:33) The result of this miracle brought many people into the

Kingdom and the Church was born in Sharon. (v.35) Then Peter went to Joppa where the Church was meeting in houses of the saints and he prayed for Dorcas, who was raised from the dead. This made the Church to grow tremendously. There was house meeting by the Church in Simon, the tanner's home.

The Church was born in the gentile country called Caesarea when Cornelius and his family came to the Lord. They met in Cornelius' house. (Acts.10:34-48) Racial tension was brewing in Jerusalem within the Apostles and the Elders, because they thought Jesus Christ was exclusively for the Jews. So when Peter came from Cornelius' home, a gentile, they took him to task and demanded for the reason why. Peter narrated his story once more and told them about the sheet let down from heaven, and the instruction by God to kill and eat.

Peter objected to the heavenly voice and the Lord told him: "What God has cleansed, you must not call common." The sheet was received into heaven after three times. When the Apostles, Elders and the Church heard what Peter had to say, they were all silent and glorified God saying: "Then God has also granted to the Gentiles repentance to life." They were totally surprised and could not believe their ears concerning what God had done. So their racial bias began to receive some fatal blows from the Spirit of God.

The persecution that scattered the Church over Stephen, made the people of God to go as far Phoenicia, Cyprus and Antioch, and they were preaching the Word to no one, but the Jews. God had already touched some Gentiles amongst them, and these saints were Gentiles, from Cyprus and Cyrene. They went to their people in Antioch and spoke to the Greeks, preaching Jesus Christ. The hand of God was with them, and many people were born into the Kingdom of God.

The second Gentile Church beside Cornelius Home was born by the Spirit of God, and they too met in homes and houses, coming together into a large place for meeting. (Acts.11:19-26) The news of the second Gentile Church came to the Apostles and Elders in Jerusalem, and they sent Barnabas to Antioch. When he saw them, he was glad and encouraged them all that with purpose of heart they should continue with the Lord. So the people of God had now included the Gentiles and the Church began to grow with an unparalleled rapidity.

They had no denominations, no committees, no raising of funds or collection of tithes to build cathedral that would house them. The leaders were happy to serve God in this capacity, and they all had their individual jobs and profession that they were engaged in. So we had Church in Cyprus, Cyrene, Antioch and many other places.

When there was famine in the land of the Jews, they collected money, goods and reliefs for them in Jerusalem. The money that the Church had was not for paying ministers, inventory, hydro, overheads, heat etc, but for the fatherless, orphans, widows, strangers and many others that were rejected by the societies. The Levites in the Old Testament who did not receive inheritance amongst the Twelve Tribes of Israel, were catered for by God Himself through the generosity of His people.

There was one thing that was very disturbing, and this was the matter: The Apostles did not want to leave Jerusalem, and they just stayed put in the city. Another wave of persecution began this time by king Herod. (Acts.12) He took James, the brother of John, and sawed him into two sending him to his grave. He saw that this pleased the Jews, and so, he proceeded to arrest Peter as well, intending to bring him out for public execution after the Passover. Peter was kept in prison under four soldiers in maximum security.

The Church organized prayer meeting all over the land, but it was Peter's house Church that was mentioned, and this was at Mary's house John Mark's mother. Prayers were going on across the Churches for Peter, unto God, that his life would not end as James' life was terminated before their eyes. They challenged God and He responded to it, setting Peter free by the hand of His angel who came to the inner cell and all the doors and gates opened to them automatically.

Peter was released by the intervention of God and the angel disappeared from him. He went to the house Church where they were gathering before his arrest, but the door could not be opened to him automatically. God will not open the doors and gates that we have invented to keep us from the world. We have to open those doors and gates by ourselves. Eventually the door was opened and Peter motioned to them to be quite. He recounted what had happened to him and how the Lord sent His angel in response to the prayers of the saints all across Jerusalem. Then he disappeared from the area beyond Jerusalem, Judea and Samaria. He got the message that the Lord had originally given to them in Acts.1:8.

He told the Church to tell James, a leader of another House Church, the brother of Jesus Christ, and the many brethren across the land. Needless to say that evil was determined against the guards when they were told to bring out the prisoner. They did not find him and they searched all the land for Peter. Meanwhile, the soldiers were executed in cold blood, and others took their place.

There was one assignment that should be carried out by the same angel who set Peter free from the tyranny of the king. Herod, the king, went down to the Caesarea and stayed there for some days. Tyre and Sidon were subjected to the king and they received their supply from his country. They hired Blastus to help them quell the anger of the king towards them, and when he was arrayed in royal regalia while sitting on the throne, the people kept shouting saying: "The voice of a god, and not that of a man!" He did not give the glory to God, and for that he was struck by the angel of the Lord, and worms devoured his body. So, king Herod died a woeful death. (Acts.12:1ff)

It was an honor for the early saints to open up their homes and houses as a meeting place where the power of God ministered amongst them. Today, we have all kinds of things we are afraid of, and therefore refused to open up our houses to God. We have the problems of litigation, death in our homes, theft, familiarity and all kinds of problems. We are not different from them, and we should not be afraid to step out for the glory of God. Do we think that we are so sophisticated, civilized, cultured, rich and famous that we cannot allow the Lord into our homes or houses?

There is something precious and unique when the saints make room for the Lord God, Almighty in their homes when they are gathered together. It is like having the Ark of the Covenant coming to the house of Obededom in 2Sam.6:10-12. When the Ark entered into his house, things changed for him, and the members of his household. The Lord's blessings, provisions and protection were upon them all. Even so, when you open your home to house the Church, you are opening it to the presence of the Lord God, Almighty. You will be protected and you will abound in blessings and provisions of the Lord. Open your homes to Jesus Christ, and to the Spirit of the Lord in this city of Winnipeg and Brandon. Do not be afraid or let your heart be troubled. He is in charge of His Family on earth, and nothing will cause you harm or litigation.

THE FEAR OF MAN
ACTS.13:1FF

Paul was a courageous and bold man, but his past and heritage hunted him for a long time, because he killed the saints of God and had them committed to prisons. God forgave him and forgot the accounts, but Paul could not erase it from his heart. If one watches carefully his journeys from Antioch to his first and second missions, and then to Jerusalem before his arrest, one will find that Paul was not free from the fear of man, even though he wrote extensively about it. No wonder a messenger of the devil was allowed of God to be in his life. God was in control and not the devil, and he was able to live with it. Although the scriptures say that the adversary of the devil came to him in order to humble him for the abundance of revelation given to him. (2Cor.12:7)

They sailed off from Antioch, sent by the Spirit of God and the Church as they laid hands on him and Barnabas. (v.4) They went to Seleucia, Cyprus and Salamis. Where did they go? They went to the Synagogue of the Jews, but he was sent to the Gentiles. (Acts.9:15-16) The first of the three places Paul was sent to was the Gentiles, but he went to the last of the three, the Jews. The Gospel had reached many Jews and besides, the Jews had many of their kinds, but not the Gentiles. (v.5)

Then they sailed to Paphos and met Jews, Bar Jesus, Sergius Paulos and the Islanders. God used him to defeat Satan's captain in Elymas, and Sergius Paulos gave his heart to the Lord when he saw the demonstration of Power by the Spirit of God. (v.12) It is very important to note that the Gentiles were not considered as part of the commonwealth of God and Israel. (Acts.11:19)

They left Paphos to Perga in Pamphy where John Mark departed from them, and went back to Jerusalem. They left Perga to Antioch in Pisidia, and this was different from the Antioch where they were sent by the Spirit of God. Again, where did they go? They went to the Jews, (vv.14-41) and faced unnecessary persecutions from them. (v.42) But the Gentiles begged them to stay, and speak to them. They agreed to spend the next Sabbath with the Gentiles and the whole city came out to hear them. But the Jews were filled with envy and rage when they saw great multitudes of the Gentiles.

Compare Acts.7 and 13:16ff. Paul and Barnabas said to the Jews, "It was necessary that the Word should be spoken to you first, but since you reject it and judge yourselves unworthy of everlasting life, behold, we turn to the Gentiles, for so the Lord has commanded us." If this was the instruction given to Paul by his Commander, the Lord Jesus Christ, why then was he going to the Jews? The fear of man was the answer. Paul even quoted the scripture saying, "I have set you as light to the Gentiles that you should be for Salvation to the ends of the earth." (Isa.49:6 and Acts.1:8)

The Gentiles were glad when they heard these words and they glorified God for as many as had been appointed unto eternal life believed. The Gospel gained ground and the word of God spread throughout the regions, but persecution came from the Jews. They stirred up the devout and prominent women, and the chief men of the city. They expelled the Apostles, but not before they shook the dust of their feet against them. The Gentile disciples were filled with joy and the Spirit of God was upon them all.

In Chapter 14, they moved to Iconium and again they went to the Synagogue to speak to their kinds: the Jews. They had a huge crowd having both the Jews and Gentiles, who believed in Christ and committed their lives to Him. But the unbelieving Jews stirred up the Gentiles and poisoned their minds against the Apostles. (v.2) However, they stayed in Iconium for a long time, speaking boldly in the Lord who was bearing witness to the Word of His grace, granting signs and wonders to be done by their hands.

But the Jews kept on stirring troubles for the Apostles and the multitudes were divided. The rulers planned to abuse and stone them, but words got to the Apostles and they fled to Lystra and Derbe, cities of the Lycaonia. As they ran, they were preaching the Gospel to the surrounding regions.

MIRACLE OF HEALING AT LYSTRA
(14:8-18)

At Lystra, they encountered a man who was born crippled from his mother's womb, and he was listening with all of his heart to the preaching of Paul. Paul saw that he had faith to be healed and therefore called out with a loud voice, "Stand up straight on your feet!" The man leaped to his feet and walked. The man that was healed was a Gentile and Paul was speaking to the crowds of Gentiles.

When the crippled man suddenly stood up on his feet and walked, the air was electrified and the people cried out saying, "The gods have come down to us in the likeness of men!" Only the gods can restore a person born from birth and since Paul and Barnabas were able to do this, they must be gods. They called Barnabas, Zeus and Paul, Hermes because he was the chief speaker. They brought oxen and garlands to the gates intending to sacrifice with the multitudes for these gods in human flesh.

The Apostles forbade them and maintained that they were just men like them. They were preachers telling the Gentiles to turn from these useless things to the Living God, who made the heaven, the earth, the sea and all things that are in them. God allowed bygone generations in all Nations to walk in their own ways. Nevertheless, He did not leave Himself without witness, in that He did good, gave us rain from heaven, with fruitful seasons and filled our hearts with food and gladness." With these sayings they were barely able to restrain them from making gods out of the Apostles.

It is worthy of note that the Gentiles who became followers of the Lord did not have structures erected for the Apostles or for themselves as a gathering place for the new converts. They followed the tradition of the Apostles and met in homes and houses of the saints. Also the hand of the Lord was upon the

Apostles when they were concentrating on the Gentiles, than when they went to the Jews, who constantly raised opposition and blockages to the advancement of the Gospel.

Troubles again came from the Jews from Iconium and Antioch in Pisidia. They persuaded the multitudes and stoned Paul, dragging him out of the city, supposing he was dead. The Jews thought that they had finally killed Paul. The writer believes that Paul was actually dead, but he was brought back to life through the prayers of the saints and the promise of God to him. He was raised from the dead. (Acts.9:16) This did not prevent him from going back to the Jews. However, they left that region in Derbe.

THE JOURNEY BACK HOME
(VV.21-28)

At Derbe, they preached the Gospel to the city and made many disciples before they returned to Antioch, where they were commended to the work and grace of God. They passed through Lystra, Iconium strengthening the souls of the saints and exhorting them to continue in the faith. They made them to understand that "we must through many tribulations, enter the Kingdom of God."

They appointed elders and leaders in the House Churches and prayed with fasting, commending and committing them to the Lord in whom they have believed. They passed through Pisidia and came to Pamphylia. They preached the Word at Perga and then went to Attalia. They sailed from here to Antioch where they had been commended to the grace of God for the work that they had completed. They gathered the Church together and reported all that God had done through them amongst the Gentiles. They spoke of how the Lord had opened the door of faith to the Gentiles. And they stayed in Antioch for a long time, and were going in and coming out with the saints.

It is important to notice that they were not talking about Church building, paying of ministers, asking the people to give their tithes, and there was no committee to do this or that. They had homes and houses where the people met in and the original leaders besides Paul and Barnabas were in their midst. God uses men and women who will make themselves available unto Him, whether among the Jews or the Gentiles. He does not have favorites, neither does He show preference towards people. God does not have grand children. In every Nation of the world, He responds to whoever fears Him and works righteousness. (Acts.10:35)

CONFLICTS: INTERNAL
(ACTS.15:1FF)

The Jewish converts still wanted to show their superiority over the Gentiles, and they maintained the racial bias and discrimination. So, they went to Antioch to trouble the saints. They had great dissention over the circumcision of the Gentile saints to the point that they had to go to Jerusalem to settle the matter, because there was an impasse in the Church at Antioch. They sent Paul and Barnabas with the accusers to the Apostles and Elders in Jerusalem, the final authority to this question. They did not pray, neither consulted with the Spirit of God, who is the Owner of the Church. In fact, they did not invite the Lord to settle the feud for them, but instead, they trusted in man before the Lord. Can you see human errors and mistakes in this matter of both the Church at Antioch, the Apostles, the Elders and the whole Church in Jerusalem?

It is of note that they still looked to the Apostles and Elders in Jerusalem, even though the Sanhedrin wanted their heads including their kings. King Herod was looking for Peter after the angel of God set him free from the tyranny of the people. Where were the Apostles and Elders? In homes and houses and when they had to come together, they met in a large or public place secretly. The Jews were going to defend Moses till the last drop of blood is drained from them and they represented a huge obstacle to the preaching of the Gospel of Christ.

Barnabas and Paul went to Jerusalem to resolve the issue of circumcision amongst the Gentiles. They passed Phoenicia and Samaria, describing the conversions of the Gentiles and caused great joy among all the saints. They arrived in Jerusalem and were received by the Church, the Apostles and the Elders. They repeated all that God had done through them, but some of the sect of the Pharisees, who believed in Christ, rose up, saying, "It is necessary to circumcise them, and to command them to keep the Law of Moses." They were determined to consummate the marriage between the OT and the NT, thus making the Salvation of Christ amongst the Gentiles to stand on the Law that was obsolete according to Hebrews chapters 5-10.

The Council was in session with the Church, the Apostles, Elders, the accusers and the messengers from Antioch. Here they would settle once and for all the circumcision of the Gentiles. (vv.6-21) One by one, they took their stand to share what God had been doing amongst them, and how He purposed to merge the Jews and the Gentiles into one man. Peter was up first and he narrated what God did in Cornelius Household, particularly mentioned the sheet let down from heaven. He concluded by saying, "God told him not to call common, what the Lord has cleansed." (Acts.15:9-11)

Then Paul and Barnabas took the stage and declared the many miracles and wonders God had done through them among the Gentiles. James took the floor, saying, "Men and brethren, listen to me: Simon had declared to us how God at first visited the Gentiles to take out of them a people for His Name and the words of the prophets agreed to it. (vv.16-19)

After this, I will return and build the Tabernacle of David that has fallen down. I will rebuild its ruins and set it up so that the rest of mankind may seek the Lord, even all the Gentiles who are called by My Name." says the Lord who does all these things. "Known to God from eternity are all His Works."

Then James said, "I judge that we should not trouble those from among the Gentiles who are turning to God. But that we write to them to abstain from things polluted by idols, from sexual immorality, from things (animals) strangled and from blood. Moses has had throughout all generations those who preached him in every city, being read in the Synagogues every Sabbath."

Note: The racial bias, discrimination and exclusivity to the Lord Christ hounded the Jewish saints, even though they were in Christ. They were Jews at heart and very loyal to the Laws of Moses.

ANANIAS AND SAPPHIRA

Chap.5: vv1-11. What was the motivation of Mr. and Mrs. Ananias to hold back portion of the sale of their possession? Was it the enemy, jealousy or lack of understanding of the Spirit of God? They exhibited effusively external joy and responded out of their heads to God, but their hearts were far from Him. Sin was at the heart of their action, and they did not know what it meant to give all to God. They did not open their hearts to the river of grace flowing from the Spirit of God. Outwardly, they presumed salvation, but inwardly they had not connected with the God of heaven, even though they were baptized.

It was very clear from what was happening here that the Spirit of God is God Himself. (v.4d) The Lord God Himself judged them and not Peter in order that all who would go the way of the Ananias, evil, sin and the enemy would learn from their experience. They both died from listening to the voice of evil. They were also guilty of insincerity, not to man, but to the

Owner of the Church, God Himself. (v.9) Great fear came upon all the Church and upon all who heard the judgment of the Spirit of God.

Note: What was the matter with Ananias and his wife? Were they thinking that this was just a child's play and the making of man? Have they convinced themselves that they could get away by doing this and giving false information? Could it be that their hearts were not for God, just as Judas Iscariot's heart was not for God, even though he was numbered with the twelve? They really believed that they could pull out this trick and go scot-free without being detected. But it was not so with the Lord who sees in darkness as if it were daylight.

This was a lesson for all of mankind that God is not mocked or deceived. It was not then and certainly not now. Whatever a man sows that will he reap, either of corruption or righteousness. It showed that it was God, not the Apostles, who was in charge of the young Church. He would not allow the Church to be desecrated and decimated with corruption at the infancy stage. There are so many things we do that we think we can get away with, but God is displeased with them, because the little foxes spoil our vines and render them unproductive. If man does not see them, we ought to know that God sees them all and so do we. Ananias and his wife, Sapphira, knew what they were doing, and God knew it too, even though the Apostles did not know. They were aware of it by the Spirit of the Lord.

Are there some negative secret things you are involved in, and you think no one knows of them? You are kidding yourself! God knows, and you know it too, and it will be well with you if you stop them and repent of your ways.

vv.12-21: Special miracles, signs and wonders were done by the Spirit of God through the Apostles to the point that Peter's shadow received the anointing of God to heal, and handkerchiefs taken from Paul body healed sick folks and demons influenced people. God added thousands to the Church and multitudes of both men and women were born into the Kingdom of God. Multitudes gathered from the surrounding cities to Jerusalem bringing sick people and those who were tormented by evil spirit and they were all made whole. What humanity was seeing were the rains of the mercy of God upon His creation, and the Lord was so present in His Church. They did not have to lay hands upon the multitudes. It was a miracle and God was amongst His people in an uncontested, tangible way. God honored the Apostles, and the people held them in high esteem. (vv.12-16)

vv.17-21: When the light is shining, with transforming power, authority and compassion, darkness is vexed and greatly agitated. The high Priest and those who were with him of the sect of the Sadducees rose up in indignation against the Church, and rounded up the Apostles, putting them in jail. But man cannot imprison God! The enemy (the devil) was so mad that he instigated the leaders and the people of Jerusalem against the Church. But God opened the locked prison cells, built by man without using keys and He said to the Apostles, "Go, stand in the Temple and speak to the people all the words of this life."

When God instructs you to do something, you better respond quickly and immediately. They went into the Temple in the morning and taught. It was God versus Satan and the powers of darkness, and both sides had their champion: the religious, political leaders on one side, instigated by Satan, and the Church, the army of God, on the other side. The battle line was drawn and the high Priest and those who were with him called the government of land, and banded together. The Elders of the children of Israel were also present. They sent to the prison to have the Apostles brought before them, not knowing that God had opened the prison doors, and set the Apostles free to minister His Word in the Temple.

The government was hostile to the Gospel, and even now, it is hostile to Christ and His saints. Yet, we go after the governments of the land for their money, income tax rebates or refund, support and whatever they have for us. In the first century, it was not so. Friendship with the world is enmity with God, and behind the governments of this world, is the enemy of God, Satan, the devil. Nothing good will come from the governments of the land taking the municipal, provincial and federal governments into consideration. If they will not receive the knowledge of God and trust in Christ, then a day of reckoning is coming, and all governments will bow at the feet of Christ for judgment.

We see the power of God and the puny and weak power of the enemy, and the two groups they were using to further their programs: the governments and the Church. One must prevail over the other, just as Christ prevailed over Satan, the enemy of God, Christ and mankind. Jesus Christ in His triumph shouted, "It is finished" and the hold over man by Satan has come to an end through the death of Christ on the cross of Calvary.

They sent the officials to the prison, which were well secured and there was no tempering with the locks. But to the amazement of the official policemen, they found no one in the cells. When it was reported to the authority, they were surprised beyond words. Meanwhile, news came to the leaders that the men that were supposed to be imprisoned, were in the temple teaching the people. The officers brought them without violence to the leaders for fear of their lives to avoid being stoned. They set the apostles before the Council and they were being questioned. They said, "Did we not command you not to speak in the name of Jesus Christ, but you have filled Jerusalem with your teaching and intending to bring Jesus' blood upon our heads?" They were untruthful to themselves, because earlier on before the Romans crucified Christ, they said, "His blood be upon us, and our children" (Matt.27:25)

Then Peter and the rest of the Apostles answered, "We ought to obey God, rather than men. The God of our fathers raised up Jesus Christ, whom you killed by hanging Him on a tree. This Jesus had God exalted to His right hand to be Prince and Savior, to give repentance to Israel and the forgiveness of sins. We are His witnesses to these things, and so is the Spirit of God, given to those who obey Him." (Acts.5:32)

THE WRATH OF MAN (INSTIGATED BY SATAN)

When the Apostles said that they would obey God, instead of man and made them culpable for the murder of the Prince of Life, whom God raised up, that He would not see corruption, the religious and political leaders were furious, and wanted to kill all the Apostles. God had a man amongst them, and the Spirit of God spoke through him. His name is Gamaliel.

He brought their attention to the past history of the Jews as they wrestled for political freedom from the Roman tyranny. He reminded them of Theudas and Judas of Galilee, who rose up respectively in the insurrection of the Jews against a cause they were opposed to. The crowds and their leaders perished. Now he said, "Keep away from these men and leave them alone. If this plan of theirs is of men, it will come to nothing, but if it be of God, you cannot overthrow it, lest you will even be found fighting against God."

They saw wisdom in what he said and refrained from killing the Apostles. Nevertheless, they had them flogged and bitten before they were released. They also told them that they were forbidden to speak the Name of Jesus.

The Apostles departed from the Council, rejoicing that they were counted worthy to suffer shame for His Name. They continued to speak daily to the people in the Temple and in every house. They did not cease to preach and teach Jesus as the Christ.

Do we know what it is to have the sentence of death hanging over our heads? The Council had agreed to kill them, but Gamaliel's words turned them away from their plot. Do you know the implication of killing all the Apostles? It would mean that Jesus' prayers were not answered and fell into deaf ears. The suffering of Christ, the shed blood and His ultimate death were in vain. It would mean that the disciples were a failure and there would be no one to carry the torch of life and salvation to the world. God would not allow that to happen and so He had the intervention of His Spirit upon Gamaliel, who apparently saved the Apostles from death. God has always existed and He is still alive in the 21st Century. He has His ministers, apostles and the Gamaliels of this world, who are creating opportunities for men and women to know God through the Spirit.

He will always frustrate the will of Satan and the evil people who are calling for the heads of the saints of God. These people are in the city Council, governments of the land, in medical fields, judiciary, business, military, police services, and wherever people oppose the will of God.

Chapter 6:1-7: External forces cannot destroy or demolish the works of God, or the things started even by man. These external forces empower the members and make them stronger, but not so with the internal forces or squabbles. They have the potential to create a devastation and untold havoc within the Church and amongst friends.

The Church was growing and multiplying in numbers, and the Hellenistic Jews started to complain about the Hebrew Jews, concerning the favoritism shown to their kind, in the administration of the foods. Persecution by the Jews and troubles in the Church had the combined ability to greatly upset and derail the young Church. Prominent among the complaints were the issues of discrimination, partiality and differentiation. They were all Jews, but distinction was made between the Hebrews and the Hellenist widows, and they were being discriminated against. They were getting away from the love of God and the sea of grace that was flowing to all. Man began to get in the way of the Spirit of God.

The Apostles knew that this was a potential trouble coming from the inside of the Church. They rallied round and came up with God's wisdom. They said, "It is not desirable that we should leave the Word of God and serve tables. Seek from within yourselves seven men of good reputation, full of the Holy Spirit and wisdom, who we may appoint over this business. But we will give ourselves continually to prayers and the ministry of the Word of God."

This wisdom resonated well in the minds of the Church and it saved nine, because it was a stitch in time. They did not allow the discrimination to fester, and it was nib in the bud, before the enemy ran with it. They chose Stephen, a man full of faith and the Holy Spirit, Philip, Prochorus, Nicanor, Timon, Parmenas and Nicholas, a proselyte from Antioch. The Church set these men before the Apostles and when they had prayed, they laid hands on them, and set them apart as deacons to serve food to the Church.

The enemy wanted to penetrate their ranks and files, but they shot the door to his face, and kept him out. This was a huge success as to how the Church would handle their affairs in the future, taking heed to the Spirit of God. The word of God spread as a result and their numbers were greatly multiplied in Jerusalem. Also a great many of the priest, were obedient to the faith, and committed their lives to Christ. The internal crisis had great potential to destroy the young Church, but the wisdom of God came through for all through the Apostles and with the Spirit's leading. The enemy was crushed!

INTERNAL & EXTERNAL CRISIS

The murderous spirit that was on the Council was temporary restrained. It surfaced here amongst the people of Israel through the five synagogues. The law was trying to creep in amongst the people of God. These five synagogues spoke lies against Stephen over three times, and they were able to instigate the Council, and a critical mass was reached. It led to the death of Stephen.

Stephen was full of faith and power. He did great signs and wonders among the people and the synagogues of the freed men were envious of him. But in fact, they were mad at God, who gave men such powers. On three occasions they bore false witness against him. (vv.11, 13 & 14) Regardless of the murderous look on their faces, Stephen's face was like that of an angel of God and, and the Council witnessed this glory on Stephen's face. (v.15)

Who was at work here? Was it God or Satan? It was God at work through His Spirit, and ministering to him against the accusation of those who wanted his head. Eventually, the mob won, and Stephen was stoned to death. Were there no Gamaliels in this situation, prepared by God to save Stephen's life? Could not God have come to rescue him from the tyranny of the mob? Where were the Apostles? Could they not have prevailed on his behalf? Men and women stay or die by the will of God! Stephen had to defend himself, and all of chapter 7 was his defense. It was Stephen's defense, but it was God's through him. God does not need to defend Himself, but once in a while, He does, and this account in chapter 7 was that divine defense. Why did Stephen die? God allowed his blood to be the ground upon which thousands were sown, and came to Jesus Christ. Saul of Tarsus was in that number.

DIVINE DEFENSE THROUGH STEPHEN

7:1-8. Stephen was not afraid of dying, because he was full of faith. People who have bowed their knees to God are never afraid of death, lions or blazing fire. Through Stephen, God recounted the history of Israel from Abraham to the present. How Israel started was not different from the rest of mankind. In fact, the whole of mankind was putrefying, sticking and polluted water. God took a cup of that rotten water as it were to His lab, and began to work on it, from Abraham to the present day in which Stephen was speaking. God told Abraham to get out of his country and his relatives, and come to a land that He would show him. (v.3) Abraham obeyed and came out of the land of the Chaldeans into Haran. At Haran, his father died, and God moved him to the Promised Land in which his descendants dwelt.

God gave him no inheritance in the land, and not even enough to set his feet on. (v.5) The promise was given to him when he had no children, yet God said He would give him the land, and his descendants after him. Then God told him that his descendants would dwell in a foreign land, and the people would bring them into bondage, oppression and slavery for 400 years. He would judge this nation, and after that, they would come out and serve Him in this place. He gave him the covenant of circumcision, and Abraham begat Isaac, Isaac begat Jacob and Jacob begat the twelve patriarchs.

vv.9-16: The patriarchs became envious and sold Joseph into Egypt because their father, Jacob loved him above them all. Joseph's dreams even made things worse. But God was with Joseph, and He made him to prosper. He delivered him from all his troubles and gave him favor and wisdom before Pharaoh, the king of Egypt. This Pharaoh made him governor over all of Egypt and his household. When God plans to do a thing through you, and His purposes are made known in your spirit, no one can kill you, because God is not finished with you yet. The only one that can sabotage that plans of God in your life is you.

Now a great famine came over all Egypt and Canaan, and Jacob found no sustenance for his family. He sent his sons to Egypt having heard that there was grain in the land. They returned with food, but when they returned to Egypt the second time, Joseph was made known to his brothers. Before long, Jacob and his family were in Egypt. There were 75 of them that came from Canaan into Egypt, and that prophecy to Abraham was fulfilled. Jacob died in Egypt, having met his beloved son, Joseph, but when it was time to leave Egypt, they carried his bones to Shechem and made his final resting place there with Abraham, Isaac and Sarah, the burial place that Abraham bought from the sons of Hamon, the father of Shechem.

vv.17-36. God delivered Israel through Moses, as terror came to the Jews in Egypt when they multiplied into millions. There arose a Pharaoh who knew not Joseph, and thus this began the end of the 400 years in oppression, bondage, terror and slavery. The king dealt treacherously with the Hebrews, oppressing and making their babies to be exposed to death through the hands of his ministers.

At this time, Moses was born, and he was well pleasing to God, and was brought up in his parents' house for three months. But when they could not hide him any longer, they gave him up and Pharaoh's daughter brought him into the king's palace, and made him her son. This Moses that Israel rejected, was chosen of God to lead them out of the tyranny of Pharaoh. He was reared in the king's court, and learned in all the wisdom of the Egyptian. He was mighty in words and deeds.

Moses at the age of 40 came to realize that he was not an Egyptian, and he visited his brothers on the field, in rigor and hard labor. He saw a Jew being maltreated by an Egyptian, and intervened by killing the Egyptian who was the oppressor. The news of his killing an Egyptian spread beyond the palace to all Egypt, and it was unknown to Moses. However, he thought that through his actions, they would understand that God would deliver them. The next day as he was visiting his people on the field of slavery, he saw two Hebrews in altercation, and he wanted to make peace between them. But the one who was in the wrong said, "Who made you a ruler and a judge over us? Do you want to kill me as you killed the Egyptian yesterday?" Then Moses fled and became a fugitive at this saying, and dwelt in the land of the Median, where he took a wife and had two sons. Another 40 years had passed, and Moses had forgotten his flight from Egypt, but God had not. When Moses was on Mount Sinia, God appeared to him in a burning bush that was not burning. He saw this wonder, and drew near to behold. Then the voice of God spoke to him saying, "I AM the God of your fathers: the God of Abraham, Isaac and Jacob. " Moses was troubled greatly as he trembled and dared not to look.

This Moses was the very one that God used in liberating His people from the tyranny of Pharaoh, and into the Promised Land. He saw it on Mount Pisgah, but he did not step his foot in it.

Chapter Twenty-Three

THE CHURCH: AN ORGANISM

NTCHURCH.ORG
By Permission

The apostle Paul wrote in Eph.5:23-32, "For the husband is the head of the wife, even as Christ is the head of the Church: and He is the Savior of the body. Therefore, as the Church is subject unto Christ, so let the wives be to their own husbands in every thing. Husbands, love your wives, even as Christ also loved the Church, and gave himself for her; that he might sanctify and cleanse her with the washing of water by the word, that he might present her to himself a glorious Church, not having spot, or wrinkle, or any such thing; but that she should be holy and without blemish.

So ought men to love their wives as their own bodies. He that loves his wife, loves himself. For no man ever yet hated his own flesh; but nourishes and cherishes it, even as the Lord the Church: For we are members of his body, of his flesh, and of his bones. For this cause shall a man leave his father and mother, and shall be joined unto his wife, and they two shall be one flesh. This is a great mystery: but I speak concerning Christ and the Church."

In this passage, we ought to be able to see and appreciate the close relationship that exists between Christ and the Church.

The close affinity between Christ and the Church is suggested by the figure of the relationship between husband and wife.

It was predicted by Isaiah, that God would give in his house "a place and a name" better than that of "sons and of daughters". (Isa.56:5) We are told in ITim.3:15, that God's house is the "Church of the living God." The term "wife" is suggestive of a closer tie and a more divine union than "sons and daughters." As the husband is the head of the wife, Paul said that even so, Christ is the head of the Church.

Therefore, the apostle Paul suggests in Eph.5:23, that the husband is Christ, and the wife is the Church. Just as a husband and a wife become one, and forsake all and any other, and blend their lives into a oneness and unity, in the same way a Christian is to forsake everything else, divorce himself from everything that would hinder, and blend his life into the life of the Lord Jesus Christ. The husband is Christ, and we, as members of the Church, make up the wife, or the bride of Christ. The marriage relationship that results is the Church of Christ, under the headship of Jesus Christ, our Lord.

I also believe there is an analogy between the first woman, who ever lived on the earth, Mother Eve, and her husband, Adam, and the Church of Christ in her relationship to Jesus Christ, our Lord.

The Bible relates, in the second chapter of Genesis, that after all the things of the earth had been created, the beasts of the field, the fish of the sea, and the fowls of the air, all these various things were brought to Adam to see by what name he would call them. When Adam had named all the beasts of the field, and all the fowls of the air, the Creator was conscious of the fact that every animal and every fowl had its respective mate, and then God looked at man, and said, "It is not good." Up until that moment, God's pronouncement had been not only that things were good, but that they were very good. But now God came to a point in the development of creation in which he said, "It is not good." What was it that was "not good"? He said: "It is not good that the man should be alone." (Gen.2:18) Probably there are a number of women, young and old, who would agree with that statement, and they are right.

God said that it was not good for man to be alone, and he said: "I will make an help meet for him." I might point out that the term "help meet" means "suitable companion." In accord with God's determination to make a help meet for Adam, the last, greatest and highest of all creation, was brought into existence when God created Mother Eve.

I want to show that the means God used in bringing about the creation of Adam's wife, formed a fitting analogy to the establishment, creation, and formation of the Church of Christ, which was to be the bride of the second Adam, Jesus Christ. What did God do? The Bible says: "And the Lord God caused a deep sleep to fall upon Adam, and he slept". (Gen. 2:21)

After God had caused Adam to sleep, he opened his side, and what a wonderful thing that suggests. The woman was not taken from Adam's head, that she might rule over him, nor from his feet, that he might trample upon her, but from out of his side, that she might be a partner and companion along the pathway of life. Then what happened?

The Bible says, "And he took one of his ribs, and closed up the flesh instead thereof ". (Gen.2:21) That which was to form the woman, was taken from Adam's side - a rib. Therefore, Adam paid the price, the price of his flesh and bone for the one who was to be his companion and helpmeet.

The woman was then created out of the material taken from his side. The Bible states: "And the rib, which the Lord God had taken from man, made he a woman". (Gen.2:22)

The woman was then given to Adam to be his wife, to take upon herself his name, to be married to him. The Bible says that God "brought her unto the man. And Adam said, This is now bone of my bones, and flesh of my flesh: she shall be called Woman, because she was taken out of Man". (Gen.2:22,23)

As a natural result of that union, children began to be born of that first pair, and the earth was to be replenished as a result. Rehearsing that account just briefly, we can say that Adam was at first alone, but God said that was not good. God determined to make a help meet, a suitable companion, for him. Therefore, Adam was put to sleep, his side was opened and the rib was taken from his side, the woman was created, and became Adam's wife, and as a result, children would be born and replenish the earth.

I believe that from that very simple story concerning the creation of woman, the first woman, we can draw a very beautiful analogy to the creation of the Church of the Lord Jesus Christ. God planned in his great wisdom that at the proper time, when man was ready to receive the truth, the Church was to be born. And just as Adam was the head of the woman, or the wife, so Christ was to be the head of the Church. Therefore, we may expect to find a fitting parallel in the establishment of the Church.

Do you remember what God did first in creating the woman? He caused a deep sleep to come upon Adam. Now look at the first thing he did in forming the spiritual wife, the Lamb's bride.

After Jesus had lived for thirty-three years, upon the earth, and had fulfilled the prophecies concerning him, he was taken at last and nailed to the cross. While suspended upon the cross from the third hour of the day, until the ninth hour, during the last three hours, a great darkness fell upon the face of the earth. It seems to me that God himself veiled his face and refused to look upon the greatest tragedy of all ages, which was being carried out. The record says that finally, the sinless Son of God bowed his head upon his guileless bosom, and yielded up the ghost, declaring: "It is finished."

While Jesus slept the deep sleep of death, a Roman soldier pierced his side with a spear, opening up the literal flesh of the body of Jesus, and in harmony with the creation of woman, there came forth from the side of Jesus that which was to purchase the Church of Christ. The Bible says: "And forthwith, came there out blood and water". (Jn.19:34) Therefore, Christ shed his blood, and with that sacrifice, He gave his blood, that he might purchase and buy the institution that was to be his spiritual bride, or the wife of the Son of God.

The apostle Paul said: "Take heed therefore unto yourselves, and to all the flock, over the which the Holy Ghost has made you overseers, to feed the Church of God, which he has purchased with his own blood". (Acts.20:28)

Look at what happened in the formation of the Church. God caused the sleep of death to fall upon Jesus. The material to build the Church was taken from his side. Jesus paid his blood. The Church, the Lamb's bride was to be brought into existence, and made a living reality. It was proper to characterize the Church as the wife, since she was married to Christ, and it was natural that spiritual children should be born of that union, and into the family. Just as it was impossible for woman to have been created before the opening of Adam's side, when that which formed her was taken out, even so, it is equally impossible for the Church to have been brought into existence previous to the shedding of the blood of the Son of God.

But someone might say: "The Bible says that Christ loved the Church and gave himself for her, therefore, she must have been in existence, or else he could not have given himself for her.

Well, it is true that Jesus had some followers, but they were not known or called his wife, and they did not become such until

Christ died, made the sacrifice, and gave himself for them. Then they became his bride, or his wife. When a young man falls in love with a young lady, he is willing to forsake his father and mother, and all things, and give himself to her and for her alone, because he loves her. But was she his wife previous to the time that he gave himself for her? She was in existence as a young lady, but not as his wife, and she did not become a wife, until he forsook all others, pledged his life, and gave himself for her.

So it was with the Church of Christ. Human beings were in existence before they were known as a Church, but they were not in existence as a bride, or as the wife of Christ, until he purchased them, and the marriage was consummated. Then they are joined unto him as a bride, over which he becomes the head, and in which his Spirit dwells, and they blend into one.

Paul said, in Rom.7:1-4, "Know you not, brethren, (for I speak to them that know the law) how that the law has dominion over a man as long as he lives?

What is Paul talking about? So long as the law of Moses was in existence, the Israelites were married to that law as their husband. If during its effectiveness, they had been married to another law, they would have been guilty of spiritual adultery, but if the 'first law was blotted out, then, they are loosed from it, and are not adulterers, though they be married to another law, or another man. Paul said: "You brethren are become dead to the law by the body of Christ, that you should be married to another."

What about others? Unto him. What him? Unto him who is raised from the dead. Not the one who walked over the hills of Judea, and the plains of Samaria in his personal ministry. Not married unto him, until he tasted death, but married unto Him that is raised from the dead. The man does not live who can find the marriage consummated between Christ and the Church previous to the resurrection of the Son of God from the dead.

But what is the object of this marriage, Paul? "That you should be married to another, even to him who is raised from the dead, that we should bring forth fruit unto God."

Now when he says fruit here, we do not understand it to mean the good works, which are to result from our union with Christ, but men and women born as the result of the marriage of Christ and the resultant Church. Let me point out that those children born outside of that wedlock and relationship would be illegal in their state.

We said all of that in order to say this: The Church, having become married to Christ, has the right to take upon herself the name of the husband, and the children that will result from that union, have the right to take the name of the husband or the head of the household, and become members of the family of God. They will also become heirs of all that Jesus has, because they are born into the family of God, and are therefore heirs of God, and joint-heirs, with Jesus Christ.

Since the Church is described as the bride of Christ, does not it seem to you that the Church should wear his name? Does it seem reasonable that Christ would come to earth, sorrow, suffer, bleed and die to establish the Church, and then the Church would dishonor Christ by refusing to wear his name, but would instead wear the name of some man? Also, we can see that since Jesus shed his blood to purchase the Church, (Acts.20:28) that if we are saved by his blood, we must be in the Church.

Is the Church essential to salvation? In reply to that question, I ask: Is Jesus' blood essential to salvation? Remember, he purchased the Church with his blood. If he gave his blood for the Church, and it is only by the blood that we can be saved, then it would seem that the Church should be worth what Jesus paid for it.

If I paid 100 dollars for a suit of clothes, the only way I would get any benefit out of the 100 dollars that I paid would be to wear the suit of clothes. In the same way, Jesus gave himself for the Church, (Eph.5:25) and purchased it with his blood, (Acts.20:28) therefore, I must be in the Church to receive any benefit from his purchase price.

We may see how Jesus looks at the Church from another thought in the New Testament. In Acts.8:3, it is said that Saul made havoc of the Church. But in Acts.9:4, Jesus asked Saul: "Why persecute you me?" Therefore, to persecute the Church is to persecute Christ. I do not believe people can honor Christ and glorify him, and at the same time downgrade and belittle the bride of Christ, which is the Church.

The Bible says that Christ is the head of the Church, (Eph. 5:23), and in Col.1:18, and 1:24 that the body of Christ is the Church. To separate the head from the body would be to destroy both. That proves that the Church is essential.

Sometimes people say: "Oh, I don't believe the Church is essential to salvation." Let me ask you, do you believe that Jesus would be the head of something that is non-essential? And the Bible also states that Christ is the Savior of the body. (Eph.5:23) If you think that the Church is non-essential, you will have to get another Savior, for Christ is said to be the Savior of the body over which he rules as head, that is, the Church. Are you a member of the Church that Jesus built?

CONCLUSION

The Church that Jesus Christ is building has never been the works of men. She is totally outside human jurisdiction, but God's Spirit is at work on and in all of His children. God has no grand sons and daughters, and Jesus Christ is the first-born Son of God by the Spirit, and we came through Him as adopted children of God. (Lk.1:35) He does not need human hands, knowledge, wisdom and understanding to build His Church. He is coming for her, as a bride without spot or wrinkle.

The Church of the living God cannot be, and must not be bits and pieces of a decaying and dying entity, or a thing that has no continuity, because of death. It cannot be a physical structure as well. The Church must be an undying entity, and one that has the power of an indestructible life, because she is connected to Jesus Christ, her Head. There may be all kinds of churches in the world, but there is indeed one Church, and all will be brought together under One Umbrella, and that is our Lord Jesus Christ, the Builder and Maker of His Church.

Jesus Christ said in His response to Peter's confession that "He was Christ, the Son of the living God." (Matt.16:18) He is building us, and we are of different shapes and sizes. Some tall, short, light, dark, but all to the specification of His Father, through the Spirit. The Church must be triumphant through Jesus Christ.

It is about time that we look no more at the Church from man's angle, but that we may borrow the lens from the Spirit of God to see what the Church is really being erected to be: The Power of God on Earth. Henceforth know we no man after the flesh: yes, though we have known Christ after the flesh, yet now know we Him no more. Therefore if any man be in Christ, he is a new creature: old things are passed away; behold all things have become new. (2Cor.5:16-17) We are one with Christ and God, and that means we are like Him in this world. The Church shall do exploits, subdue kingdom, bring righteousness, obtain promises, stop the mouths of lions, quench the violence of fire, escape the edge of the sword, out of weakness be made strong, wax valiant in fight, turn to flight the army of the aliens..." (Heb.11:33-40)

Human beings were in existence before they were known as a Church, but they were not in existence as a bride, or as the wife of Christ, until He purchased them, and the marriage was consummated. Then they are joined unto him as a bride, over which he becomes the head, and in which his Spirit dwells, and they blend into one.

For the woman that has a husband, is bound by the law to her husband so long as he lives; but if the husband be dead, she is loosed from the law of her husband. So then if while her husband lives, she be married to another man, she shall be called an adulteress: but if her husband be dead, she is free from that law; so that she is no adulteress, though she be married to another man. Wherefore, my brethren, you also are become dead to the law by the body of Christ; that you should be married to another, even to him who is raised from the dead, that we should bring forth fruit unto God."

Acts.7: Stephen recounted the story of how the Hebrew Nation began, and the Lord God was at the center of it all. It started with God calling Abraham out from his country and people. Then he had a son, called Isaac, and Isaac had Jacob, and Jacob had the 12 patriarchs. That was how God began with one man, and made millions of them to form a Nation. God wanted to do the same for the Church, and filled the whole world with His people. This ideal in the mind of God was on for the first 100 years, but it quickly changed when men noticed the power and the money that could come out of it.

The saints of God began to erect buildings that took the personality, form and the name of the Church, and this gave rise to mega buildings, physical structures, glass-cathedrals of the modern world. But the Church of God met in homes and houses of the saints. Contrary to the mega Churches of today, the words of the Lord stood opposed to our world. He said, "Fear not little flock, it is your Father's pleasure to give you the Kingdom." (Lk.12:32) **God does not dwell in the temple built by human hands. (Acts.7:44-50)** This should give us a clue as to what we do with structures that we have built to ourselves.

If God intended Moses to act as he was doing, could He not give him strength for it? Certainly He could. But this history illustrates something most serious. Moses is a type of Christ. Should believers be content to have other people settle the problems they consider small, and only bring the great things to the Lord? No! We should go directly to the Lord with every occasion of need. **The introduction of intermediaries is the legal principle of human organization.** No wonder we find God introducing the law of Moses in Exodus 19, and God Himself putting Israel under a form of organization that Peter later spoke of as "a yoke — which neither our fathers nor we were able to bear." (Acts.15:10)

But even among Christians, the natural tendency of our hearts is to revert to legal bondage in some way, and we fail to realize that **human organization in the Church of God is legal bondage**. Where some people are put in special places, then others do not need the spiritual exercise of being in the Lord's presence to receive guidance, for they get their guidance from human sources.

How could you accommodate such a foolish germ? You could not. Supposing the germ said, "But I want a personal relationship with you; I do not want to trust in the organizational arrangement of your body; I want to live with you." Could you offer the germ any hope of consolation? No, apart from your body, the germ cannot partake of you. Similarly, apart from the Church, one cannot partake of Christ and of his spiritual blessings. (Eph.1:6,7; 2:16,19-22; 3:6)

The Churches in the New Testament did not have names. They were only referred to according to the city they were in. Giving a name to a group is probably the biggest thing that changes the Church into an organization. (Refer to "One Church in a City") With a name, we create an identity that is separate from others, thus we change the organism into an organization. A checking account, a Church bulletin, a board of directors, by-laws, and documented membership lists are all things that create an organization. There are many more things that can do this as well, thus we follow the world in its ways, forsake the ways of Christ by building for ourselves a tower whose height will reach heaven, and make a name for ourselves. (Gen.11:4) Fear was the reason in Genesis for wanting what man made, rather God's.

Jesus Christ, John, the Baptist, the apostles and the prophets of God had to be sent first by God, and the Church must recognize what God has sanctioned. Moses was sent by God to the Hebrews in Egypt. (Exo.3:10) John was sent by God to the Israelites to be His Son's forerunner in preparation for the redemption of humanity. (Jn.1:6) Jesus Christ was sent by His

Father to humanity to be the Savior of the world. (Jn.3:16) The apostles, Barnabas and Saul were sent by the Spirit of God to the Gentile world. (Acts.13:2-3) The Scriptures say, **"How can they preach unless they are sent?" You cannot send a building, you can send a person, a corporate being like the Church.** (Rom.10:15)

Denominations came to be because of human need, and not divine need. But the fact that these people gave themselves a name, is an expression of a deeper problem. **They did not see that the true Church is an organism and not an organization.** They could only think in terms of organization, the main reason probably being that all other Christian groups have the form of an organization. So giving a name to a Church is very much a sign that we have an organization in front of us.

The key to understand an organism is to see that an organism has only one head, and not two or more. Everything is directed from this head. In the Church of God, this head is Jesus Christ. And to understand this main characteristic of an organism – (to have only one head) - is to understand unity. An organism that has more than one head is a monster. If every member focuses on Jesus, then we have unity. If certain members start to focus on something else, like men - I follow Peter, I follow Apollos, I follow Paul, I follow Luther, I follow Calvin - or organizations, that are out growing of this urge to follow men - then we have the unity disturbed.

BIOGRAPHY

I attended Christ for the Nations in 1975 to '76, and graduated with honors with an Associates of Arts Degree in Dallas, Texas. Graduated from Winnipeg Bible College and Providence Seminary with a BA and Master of Ministry Degrees.

Married to Choice and we had four children: Praise, Israel, Emmanuel and Rhema. Served as a minister under Rev. Benson Idahosa, Rev. JBS Coker and as a Director of All Nations For Christ Bible College. I also pastored several Churches from 1976-1983.

I served as a minister with the Tabernacle of Lord for 22 years, and founded the Street Love Incorporated in 1988. Was awarded the Order of Manitoba in 2012, and Caring Canadian Award in 2008.

I now live in Winnipeg with my wife, and are helping with the care of the grand children, writing books, and fellowshipping in a local congregation. This book is my sixth one.

BIOGRAPHY

www.ingramcontent.com/pod-product-compliance
Lightning Source LLC
LaVergne TN
LVHW091250080426
835510LV00007B/195